Where Salmon Come to Die

October 30, 1993

To Bernie & Sherri —
From the man who
hugged the salmon &
bugged the bears,
I hope you enjoy
this chronicle from
the Alaskan wilds.

— Leon K.

Where Salmon Come To Die

An Autumn on Alaska's Raincoast

Leon Kolankiewicz

PRUETT

PRUETT PUBLISHING COMPANY
BOULDER, COLORADO

© 1993 by Leon Kolankiewicz III

ALL RIGHTS RESERVED. No part of this book may be reproduced without written permission from the publisher, except in the case of brief excerpts in critical reviews and articles. Address all inquiries to: Pruett Publishing Company, 2928 Pearl Street, Boulder, Colorado 80301.

Printed in the United States
10 9 8 7 6 5 4 3 2 1

Library of Congress Cataloging-in-Publication Data

Kolankiewicz, Leon J.
   Where salmon come to die : an autumn on Alaska's raincoast / Leon Kolankiewicz.
     p. cm.
   ISBN 0-87108-829-0 (hc : acid-free)
   1. Kolankiewicz, Leon J. 2. Biologists—Alaska—Chichagof Island—
Biography. 3. Environmentalists—Alaska—Chichagof Island—
Biography. 4. Coho salmon—Alaska—Chichagof Island. 5. Natural
history—Alaska—Chichagof Island. I. Title.
QH31.K65A3 1993
639.9'092—dc20
  [B]   93-2167
                                      CIP

Cover and book design by Jody Chapel, Cover to Cover Design, Denver, Colorado
Cover calligraphy by Kathy McAffrey

For my father

Salmon

Nobler beasts there are by far,
  Responding to Nature's quest,
But few must heed the harsh decree —
  Giving life must end in death.

To reach this place at last,
  The ocean's danger they survived,
Eluded the bear's quick paws,
  And escaped the eagle's eye.

The salmon come by thousands,
  Their instincts drive them on,
To reach a shallow, lonely stream,
  Then rest, content, and spawn.

Above a stony, gravel bed,
  Far from mankind's eye,
Where life begins for some,
  Where salmon come to die.

Lee Kolankiewicz, Jr.

Preface

In the summer of 1982, the Alaska Department of Fish and Game posted the following job announcement in Juneau:

This position is stationed for several months in a remote field camp with few or no opportunities to return to town. Poorly heated tents, rainy, wet weather, floods, working on weirs in flood conditions, working in cold water with a wet-suit and snorkle, handling and tagging adult salmon, occasional heavy lifting of weir materials, biting insects and occasional contact with brown (grizzly) and black bears are all involved.

Sound appealing? Believe it or not, the department received scores of eager replies to this notice, my own among them. I wasn't at all sure if I had a shot at the job.

My comfortable youth in the affluent suburbs of Pittsburgh, Pennsylvania, had not exactly qualified me to run an isolated salmon weir in the Alaskan wilderness. I had timidly backed out of the Cub Scouts even before initiation, and the nearest I ever came to roughing it was an ill-fated expedition to our backyard patio one night.

Unrolling our sleeping bags side by side, my brother and I boldly climbed in and zipped up, determined to outlast the darkness and greet the dewy dawn outdoors. But our bags were adorned inside with patterns of ducks in flight rather than stuffed with real duck or goose down; they were more appropriate for indoor slumber parties than for actual camping. In any event, neither the bags nor their tender occupants were any match for the rain that ambushed us at 2:00 A.M. Cold, soggy, and dispirited, we scampered for the basement door and shut outdoor adventure behind us. It was my first brush with the capricious side of Mother Nature.

Nevertheless, I was enthralled by what I took to be wild nature: the old fields, second-growth forest, and abandoned strip mines just beyond the spreading tentacles of suburbia. The largest mammal that had managed to survive hunters and suburbanization there was the cottontail rabbit, but to me these modest woods were still wilderness, and they were my playground.

I would roam alone for endless hours under the leafy canopy every summer, swinging a stick and mowing down ranks of hapless Mayapples. In my boyhood reveries, tainted by the Cold War, I was a fighter pilot like my uncle and these delicate plants were invading enemy troops. My stick sliced through their slender stalks like withering machine gun fire. In a less destructive vein, each winter I marveled at the sight of bare woods humped under deep snow; the white branches seemed like the bleached bones of an enchanted dinosaur graveyard.

In the ensuing years at college I did gain a certain amount of outdoor experience as well as an education in natural resources management. Thus, when the leading candidate for the salmon weir position took another job, my bosses-to-be, Phil Gray and Leon Shaul, fishery biologists with Alaska Fish and Game's Coho Research Project, settled on me. Little did they realize how ignorant I was of chain saws, outboard motors, generators, two-way radios, firearms, basic carpentry, and other job prerequisites, not to mention salmon! More than once I gave them cause to doubt their selection.

Just what is a salmon weir? Basically, it's a temporary fence with one opening that is installed across a salmon stream. As the fish migrate in from the ocean or out to it they pass one by one through the opening, which allows them to be counted with some accuracy.

Although I would be the only salaried Fish and Game employee at the project, the isolation and hazards of the weir site made it too risky to send me alone. I was to be provided with an unpaid partner—a volunteer willing to work in the Alaskan wilds for nothing in order to experience the wilderness firsthand, or because it was a way to get a foot in the door with Fish and Game. At the time I was hired, my bosses Phil Gray and Leon Shaul were in the process of selecting somebody from a list of more than a dozen potential volunteers. When I saw how many people were willing to do this work for no material compensation other than food, I felt lucky to have been awarded the paid position. Volunteer Dan Hutchins* helped set up the operation and

---

*I have changed Dan's name in order to protect his privacy.

kept me company for the first three weeks. Detlef Büttner then settled in with me for the long haul to the bitter end in November's ice and snow.

The project site was a mountain-rimmed lake beside a bay called Ford Arm on Chichagof Island, eighty air miles southwest of Juneau, Alaska's capital. Topographic maps indicated the lake had never been assigned a name, and I would just as soon it stay that way. Once a place is named—loses its anonymity—it forsakes some of its wild soul. Naming is the first step toward civilizing. Yet for the sake of our project (which did after all represent a tiny incursion of civilization), we needed to call the lake something, so we settled on, simply, "Ford Arm Lake."

In a state where even the capital itself can be reached only by plane or ship, perhaps the fact that access to Ford Arm Lake was limited to floatplane is not that remarkable. Still, Juneau had a population of twenty thousand and Ford Arm Lake zero, unless brown bears were included in the census. Our resupply and mail delivery would be every two to three weeks, also by floatplane. Our only communication with civilization would be by a single-side band (two way) radio, which, it turns out, was often out of order, completely severing contact for weeks at a time.

Chichagof is one of the storm-battered outermost islands in the rugged cluster, known as the Alexander Archipelago, that comprises southeastern Alaska. "Southeast," as it is affectionately dubbed by residents, is more widely known as the Alaska Panhandle in the lower 48.

Chichagof borders the brooding Gulf of Alaska itself. Whereas other parts of the Great Land are very cold, here it is very wet. Ankle-high rubber boots are known as "Sitka sneakers." (Sitka, population five thousand or so, forty miles to the south on Baranof Island, was the town nearest to us.) Dense ancient forests of huge, mossy Sitka spruce and western hemlock cloak most of Chichagof.

Formerly, except for lakes, the only unforested areas were muskegs and alpine tundra, two natural plant communities. In recent years, however, logging clearcuts have made their unfortunate appearance. I was relieved to discover that the Ford Arm area lay within the West Chichagof-Yokobi Wilderness of the Tongass National Forest. Barring some unforeseeable change of heart in Congress (or whatever replaces that institution in the far future), trees that were already ancient before I was born might live still for centuries after I die.

Briefly, the purpose of the weir project was to arrive at an accurate count of the coho salmon "escapement." This is the number of returning adults that succeed in escaping thousands of nets and hooks (to say nothing of natural perils) to arrive back at their own watershed and spawn. The escapement estimate, supplemented by data from other sources, is used to derive the harvest rate for this particular run of cohos. Information from a number of sites is then compiled to estimate the overall harvest rate for this species in the entire region.

The ultimate aim is the optimal management of the fishery—when and where to permit the greatest number of fish to be caught without impairing future productivity, a goal resource managers call "sustained yield."

Additional data our project was to gather concerned the abundance of other salmon stocks in the system (pink, sockeye, and chum); samples of fish scales that fishery biologists could use to determine age or potentially to distinguish this coho stock from others; the timing and location of cohos spawning in the system; and the presence of marks/scars on cohos that might indicate damage inflicted by the Asian deep-sea gill-net fleet.

The coho salmon (*Oncorhynchus kisutch*), principal subject of these chronicles, is an extraordinary fish. Hatching in early spring, the coho emerges into the watery world an orphan; its parents died after spawning the autumn before. In a salmon's upbringing, instinct takes the place of parental example. Even if it could know loneliness, the orphaned coho would not, for hundreds or even thousands of siblings hatch with it. Only ten, on the average, out of these glistening multitudes will survive to spawn themselves.

In the high floodwaters of the previous October, their mother had dug a cavity, or *redd*, in the gravel with several powerful movements of her tail. Her mate—their father—hovered close at her side. Then, shuddering together in something akin to a sexual climax, eggs and milt were squirted simultaneously into the hole. All but a few evaded the mouth of a cutthroat trout that darted in out of nowhere before the male chased it away.

The following March or April, thousands of tiny coho wriggle out from the clean gravel of a clear, cold brook. For the first one to three years they dwell not here but among the horsetails and water lilies growing in the calmer water of nearby shallow ponds, sloughs, and marshes. The best coho systems have these wetlands, which serve as nurseries.

During this time the "fingerling" cohos grow slowly. They feed on tiny insects and larvae and try to avoid becoming meals themselves for Dolly Varden and trout. Only the fittest and luckiest survive these preliminary elimination rounds in the great contest to leave a legacy by perpetuating their genes. Then, one spring when they have reached about four inches in length, the cohos' scales turn silvery; simultaneous physiological changes inside prepare them to withstand salt water. By the tens or hundreds of thousands, these "smolts" migrate downstream and embark on a journey into the North Pacific, a journey from which only about one in ten will ever return.

The coho and other Pacific salmon are celebrated, even revered, because of the remarkable biological facts surrounding this oceanic odyssey. The first concerns their prodigious growth in size and weight. After barely sixteen months in the ocean, the coho's weight has increased four-hundredfold. After a comparable growth spurt, a hundred-pound human adolescent would crush the scale at almost forty thousand pounds.

Another amazing fact, a mystery really, is how the great schools of salmon are able to navigate home again, across featureless leagues of open sea. They find the way back from distant feeding pastures in the vast North Pacific more than a thousand miles away. Scientists believe that, out at sea, the salmon may orient themselves by the earth's magnetic poles. Close to the coast again, it is thought they may actually be able to *smell* their home stream, distinguishing its unique chemical signature from hundreds of others.

Home again, this last phase of their lives lasts at most a couple of months. Unlike the Atlantic salmon (which is really a trout) and other anadromous fish, which can make two or more trips to sea, the Pacific salmon have come home for good. They will never return to the ocean.

Back in the fresh water, the coho salmon undergo one final irreversible metamorphosis: They turn from silver to a deep red, and the males grow hooked snouts and protruding teeth in preparation for the literal and figurative climax of their lives. In this short-lived sexual prime they are glorious specimens, like attractive young men and women decked out for a prom.

Then, having begotten their offspring and tucked them safely to sleep for the winter under a bed of gravel, even these hardy fish at last yield their tenacious hold on life. Survivors of so many previous external dangers, they succumb to forces beyond their control or reckoning—ironically, to their own genetically programmed self-destruction. Their progeny provided for, they themselves are expendable. By the thousands, they perish in a rite of autumn. This time, there are no survivors.

The other protagonist of this story is equally legendary—the grizzly, or brown, bear. At one time, zoologists considered the Alaskan brown bear (*Ursus middendorffi*) and the grizzly bear (*Ursus horribilis*) to be separate species. The former was larger and inhabited an area confined to the rugged southern coast of Alaska. The latter ranged all the way from the Rocky Mountains of Montana and Wyoming up through western Canada into interior and northern Alaska. But taxonomists eventually realized the artificiality of this distinction—a grizzly from British Columbia crossing a stream into Alaska immediately became a brown bear—so now grizzlies and brownies are lumped into the same species, known as *Ursus arctos*. (The grizzly of the Rockies can still be differentiated as *U. arctos horribilis*, a subspecies, or race.) I use "grizzly" and "brown bear" interchangeably throughout this book.

A true wilderness denizen, the grizzly has retreated before the inexorable march of the insatiable white man across the continent. "Progress" filled up its wide-open country with settlers, livestock, and guns. Nowadays, growing towns and herds of automobiles replace the herds of bison on which grizzlies once preyed.

For thousands of years *Ursus arctos horribilis* reigned supreme over most of the American West. Yet by the late twentieth century just a few hundred harassed, micromanaged grizzlies remained in the lower 48, huddled in several mountainous pockets of the Northern Rockies. A number are wired to transmit signals on their every movement via radio collars. On the entire North American continent, the grizzly perseveres in something resembling its original presence only in the enduring wilderness expanses of western Canada and Alaska.

The brown bear's lesser cousin, the black bear (*Ursus americanus*), has not exactly flourished under the white man's reign, but it has accommodated itself to the new reality better than has the grizzly. Although brown bears can sometimes appear black, and black bears can vary all the way from cinnamon to blue in color, there are other ways of telling them apart. And it just might be important to know which it is you see approaching you ominously, raised nose sniffing the air to determine just what *you* are. As the saying goes, if you run into a black bear it'll climb a tree, but if you run into a grizzly, *you'd* better climb the tree!

However, we didn't have to worry about whether or not to start climbing—for reasons they still haven't explained to biologists, all bears on Chichagof are grizzlies. Unfortunately, none of the trees in the deep forest had any branches for climbing, so we could not escape an enraged bear this way. To be honest, I wasn't really sure what I'd do if a bear charged. Advice from the experts ranged from simply standing one's ground to running downhill, at which bears are supposedly awkward. Then there was the 12-gauge shotgun and heavy lead slugs Alaska Fish and Game provided us with.

One Friday night a decade earlier, I was attending a high school football game in the Pittsburgh suburb of Mount Lebanon. To keep me company during the game's duller moments I had brought a copy of Andy Russell's classic book *Grizzly Country*, which I have to confess captivated me more than did the athletic event at hand. During a lull in the action, one of my buddies noticed the book. To Dick it was peculiar enough that anyone would carry a book, of all things, to a football game. But when he asked me to show him the title, he burst into guffaws—what could be more ludicrous than reading about wild grizzly country during a football game in Suburbia, USA? Yet within a decade, Dick, I was no longer just reading about grizzlies.

My father, Lee Kolankiewicz, Jr., first compiled my long letters home from the Alaskan wilds into a booklet under the present title. Later, I wove in excerpts from the official log I kept for the Alaska Department of Fish and Game. Together, the two furnish some insight into what has to be one of the most unusual jobs in North America. At present, here in Southern California with its crowds, smog, and clogged freeways, I realize all the more poignantly just how unique this experience was. It seems like it belongs to another century . . . or another planet.

After the sun has set, I find my eyes drawn heavenward toward the evening star, which of course is not a star at all but our sister planet, Venus. This sublime beacon and a few of the brighter stars, such as Sirius and Rigel, manage to pierce the veil of smog and glare that now blights Southern California.

As I gaze on their ethereal splendor, for several all-too-fleeting moments I am transported back to Alaska, where I also gazed longingly at the evening stars that twinkled cheerfully over Ford Arm Lake on the rare occasions weather was fair. Closing my eyes, I can still see ghosts of the past. In front of me a river swarms with salmon fulfilling their death wish, and a brown bear on the opposite bank is peering intently into the water for its next meal. Behind, a lantern-lit wall-tent glows softly in the deepening gloom beneath the ancient trees.

Santa Ana, California
June 1991

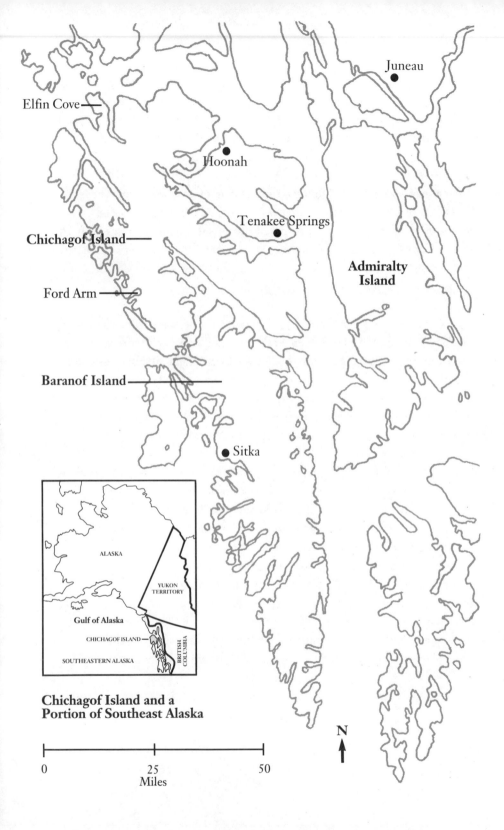

Juneau

Elfin Cove

Hoonah

Tenakee Springs

Chichagof Island

Ford Arm

Admiralty Island

Baranof Island

Sitka

ALASKA

YUKON
TERRITORY

Gulf of Alaska

CHICHAGOF ISLAND

BRITISH
COLUMBIA

SOUTHEASTERN ALASKA

**Chichagof Island and a
Portion of Southeast Alaska**

0   25   50
        Miles

N

Prelude:
Anxious Moments on the Eve of My Departure for Chichagof Island

Juneau, Alaska
July 31, 1982

Dear Folks,

I have spent the last several days shopping for the tools and equipment we are going to need for the project. We will be leaving by seaplane quite soon, a matter of a day or two.

I must tell you about the man selected to be my partner. His name is Dan Hutchins. Dan certainly deserves notice, for he is not an ordinary personality. My first impression of him (like everybody else's) was very negative. In this period prior to departing from Juneau, Dan walked into the office to apply for the volunteer opening as my unpaid partner. I did not speak to him then but still was put off by his manner and his appearance.

He smoked. He didn't smile once at anyone, and he didn't look over to me at all to acknowledge my presence. His face was dark, lean and tough, with drawn cheeks. His hair was about the length of a Marine's just out of boot camp.

The resemblance he bore to the assassin in the movie *Apocalypse Now*, or better yet to Charles Manson, didn't escape me. When my boss told me he was a Vietnam veteran, the association was strengthened and my unease increased. However, the two boss biologists assured me he was last on their list, that they too had their doubts not only as to the compatibility of Dan's personality with another's, but also as to his ability to record data reliably. This they deduced from the sparse information he supplied on his application form. For example, they are unable to check on references, one of whom was listed simply as "Butch," no last name, no phone number, no address.

My boss Leon Shaul—who is about my age—jokingly referred to Dan as "the jailbird," suggested by his shaved head and rugged looks. [I would discover later that he had in fact been thrown in jail once.] Shaul's boss, Phil Gray, who even then realized he would have to take Dan on because no other volunteers were available on such short notice, preferred to adopt a more generous view. He said Dan looked "woodsy."

Here now, just a couple of days before departure, I was seriously dismayed to find that Dan would in fact be going with me. "Utterly bummed out" may be even more apt. They simply couldn't get anyone else who could leave this soon. Leon told me that Phil, just as he picked up the phone to give Dan the go-ahead, said in a serious tone, "Well, I just hope he don't kill anybody." I, of course, was that "anybody." I was not amused, nor was the remark intended to be amusing. The fact that Leon told me at all, though, and that I did manage a laugh at least for him to see, shows that we knew we were surmising a lot about Dan's character from pretty thin evidence. Now if, on top of this, my girlfriend hadn't just dumped me last night, I might actually be able to face the unknown with a grin instead of a grimace!

You won't be hearing from me again until well after we are settled at Ford Arm Lake. The first few weeks are expected to be hectic. Long work days will be spent setting up camp and building the weir. I'll write as soon as I can.

Love,
Leon

August

August 14

2 P.M. water temp. 57 degrees F
5 P.M. air temp. 56 degrees F

Weather: overcast & drizzling, low cloud ceiling in morning; lifting skies and partly sunny afternoon. This is the second day in a row I've noticed that the clouds seem to break up & disappear in a blue sky just east of the lake (Ford Arm L.). If we were just 3 miles to the east, we'd be tanning instead of rusting!

Until today I've been too busy with getting this operation set up to record a journal entry. I'll try and recap what's happened since we arrived on August 9.

We flew to Chichagof from Juneau in typical coastal weather—mixed rain and cloud. At one point we'd been in a blank white void for a number of minutes. Only my calm stomach assured me that we were flying horizontally. I trusted the pilot could find the altimeter among the arrays of identical-looking dials on the instrument panel!

Suddenly, we burst into the open a mere hundred feet above the crest of a mountain. There, loping along the bare ridge was a hefty brown bear, its shaggy coat rippling with each stride. The noisy plane must have interrupted its afternoon stroll. It seemed significant that we should see a grizzly even before we landed. I hoped it wasn't headed our way, grumpy and bothered now.

Fortunately, the rain and whiteout receded as we arrived at the weir site. We zoomed over a forest-clad ridge and there was a kidney-shaped lake far below. From studying the topo maps I recognized it immediately as Ford Arm Lake. It appeared tiny and sunken between the mountains. The descent was dizzying! We dropped in what seemed like a free-fall; my stomach practically leapt out of my mouth. The pilot miscalculated on our first landing attempt and we had to buzz through a narrow gap (skimming the tree tops!) and out over Ford Arm to try again the other way. Beyond I could see the wide open Gulf of Alaska.

I was relieved when the plane's floats finally skidded on the surface and water splashed around us. As we puttered toward the shore, however, I felt unease envelop me again as I scanned the somber green forest. It looked brooding rather than inviting. What hidden beasts might be resentfully observing our intrusion at this very moment?

Spent the rest of the day unloading and sorting through gear (a hopeless task).

August 10

Before we'd started work the next morning we sighted a bear crossing the stream just 30 yards from camp. It looked young and skinny: more like a greyhound than a brownie. Definitely different from the heavyset one yesterday. (Just as well, if that one was still grumpy!) It looked at us as it crossed but seemed pretty nonchalant. Later that afternoon we spotted yet another bear munching on the hillside across the stream from camp. May have been the same.

Phil decided on a site for the weir and we began prepping the tripods and hauling them into the water; used all but two. Weir about 150 feet long (I believe). We spent the bulk of a long day at this. Quit at 8 P.M. Had dinner, talked, and read a few moments before crashing out.

August 11

Continued working on tripods, straightening them out, placing sandbags around, fixing up pipe and channels. Had some difficulty lining everything up and getting channels to rest flush against each other. Worked till about 8 P.M. again.

August 12

Phil was unable to reach Juneau or Sitka on the radio, despite the good weather. He was thus unable to cancel his flight out, which he had decided to do because we need more time to finish the weir. We spent some of his remaining time going over equipment (e.g., radio and accessories) and work plans until he could return, and some time working on weir. His chief admonition concerning the radio: Keep it dry!

The pilot arrived promptly and Phil took off with him. Dan and I sand-bagged the rest of the afternoon and started anchoring before quitting for the day.

August 13

Spent the better part of the day setting up anchors, of which there are eight. I put the wet suit on to be able to pound in pipes with abandon. Later went snorkeling for an hour in late afternoon. In about 3–4 feet of water right where the lake begins to open up (near all the exposed and submerged rocks just up from camp), there are roughly 20–30 sockeyes [salmon], maybe more, milling around. With snorkel and wet suit I could swim up to within several feet of them. Seemed to be a few more males than females. Also saw what may have been a couple of individuals of another species of salmon. Couldn't identify; not red; no hooked snout.

August 14

Got to it a bit later than normally. After all, this is a Saturday. (I'm still thinking in civilized terms.) Dan polished off a couple of anchors while I inserted pickets. By the time we quit in late afternoon, we had closed off the stream. Haven't put a trap in because I want Phil's on-the-spot advice while we do so.

During a break, while we stood at the "kitchen" in full view of the weir, we spotted a bear on the opposite bank, just 10 yards downstream of the weir itself. This was definitely a different specimen from the one we saw several days ago. Still appeared fairly small (to me) but had more the classic grizzly figure: heavyset (but not fat), solid, hump over shoulders. Was dark chocolate brown color. It ignored our admiring comments and walked along the bank downstream, in no hurry, seemingly undisturbed.

We took a spin up the lake for an hour or two in the late afternoon. It's a beautiful lake. Saw a couple of pairs of what seem to be common mergansers. Walked up one of the feeder streams about 200 yards. Good gravel; crisscrossed with large, ancient logs—at least one decorated with claw marks. Saw a deer and maybe mink tracks along stream. No sign of spawning salmon.

Our meat is thawed and I'm worried we'll either get sick or waste some.

Have had little opportunity to look over Leon's instructions for sampling and fish handling, etc. Will try to look at them tonight.

August 15   8 A.M. air temp. 53 degrees F

                                        3 P.M. water temp. 57 degrees F

                                        8 P.M. air temp. 54 degrees F

Finished pickets *all* the way across today (including high and dry areas). We put in some chicken wire and sandbags at either end of the weir in anticipation of higher water. It's difficult to imagine it swirling past, ripping out earth that now seems so dry and fixed.

We heard several distant gunshots early in the afternoon that seemed to come from down the valley. (Two days ago, I now recall, we heard a single *loud* shot just down-valley. Saw no one.) Hunter after deer? Bear shot in midcharge? Assassination? Suicide? War? Dunno.

Dan felled a tree (dead) that we hope to make posts out of for the wall-tent.

I haven't seen any fish backed up behind our weir yet. Dan says he's seen some that look like chums. I've seen several salmon (sockeye?) in front of it (upstream).

Later in the afternoon I took a hike downriver to tidewater. En route I saw a couple of pockets of chum salmon. Also saw 2 or 3 pinks. At tidewater, just where a tidal meadow opens to the right as you face downstream, I saw perhaps 100–200 or more chums milling about. Or were they spawning? Since I've never seen spawning salmon, I don't know how to tell the difference. Do they pair up discreetly or is it one mass orgy? They were above the tide, but below where I believe high tide would be.

August 16   8 A.M. air temp. 51 degrees F

                                        8 P.M. air temp. 52 degrees F

                                        7 P.M. water temp. 56 degrees F

Weather: socked in all day; mountain at end of lake scarcely visible. Misting much of day; raining in evening.

The water level is still down, so I took advantage of it and dug some gravel for sandbags. These I placed on the far side, where they can be used to fortify the weir bank when the need arises. There are now 35 bags over there.

Dan spent most of the day cutting and peeling logs and procuring firewood. He's anxious to start the wall-tent, but I wanted to wait for Phil (due tomorrow).

Phil asked me to tune in the radio at 3 P.M. to go over what he should bring tomorrow. I did, but got nothing from Juneau. I tried establishing contact to no avail. If tomorrow the weather is like it is now, he might not make it.

A small, plainly colored wren (I think) kept me company and sang along as I broadcast to Juneau this morning. A camp mascot? Better a wren than a bear.

Over & out . . .

August 17

8 *A.M. air temp. 51 degrees F*
8 *P.M. air temp. 54 degrees F*
5 *P.M. water temp. 57 degrees F*

Weather: started raunchy with heavy clouds & frequent downpours in morning

By 4 P.M. when Phil arrived from Sitka it had turned lovely. He remarked, of course, "Waddaya mean you never get sun around here?" His story of sweltering sunshine in Juneau for the Salmon Derby confirmed my suspicion that we are indeed in the opposite of a rain shadow, whatever that's called (a sun shadow?). And to think the water's low! Pray tell how much it'll have to rain to raise the river to what it's supposed to be in the fall!

We spent the morning clearing brush and alders from the campsite, upstream, side of the weir. After Phil arrived, he and Dan went to work on the new design Phil has for a weir-trap where we will net and sample the fish.

Phil restocked our food, emphasizing his favorites: meat and frozen juices. What a carnivore!

Well, well, well—I could say more about my philosophy of life and the path of the Zen Master, but I'll save it for another day, eh?

P.S. Bugs still bugging us.

P.P.S. Tried fishing the lake last night. Bugs bit, fish didn't.

August 18

8 A.M. air temp. 51 degrees F

9 P.M. air temp. 52 degrees F

Weather: high overcast; didn't rain all day; water very low

While Phil pounded and cut away on two sides for a trap, Dan and I endured a long, very frustrating day starting to construct the wall-tent frame: pounding nails, cutting boards, taking measurements, lining things up, then pulling nails, piecing together boards, retaking measurements, and repounding nails. We scarcely nailed one board to another that we didn't have to rip out again — two steps backward for each forward.

At day's end, however, after a classic display of *ad hoc* carpentry, we had a frame that rested reasonably level on a number of log supports — and a floor of plywood on the frame without too many cracks between sections, or too much bounce like a gym floor when you walk across it.

The bugs are pressing in on me, as is the darkness, so I'll call it quits for now.

August 19

8 A.M. air temp. 49 degrees F

7 P.M. air temp. 59 degrees F

Weather: gorgeous all day, further discrediting my complaints to Phil about the raunchy weather!

A *very* long and wearisome day spent on the tent platform setting up the frame. More problems with things not lining up. Difficulty in understanding *why* things aren't lining up. Makes you feel like a real dumbo.

At day's end we had the studs and walls up and were working on putting the rafters together. Couldn't figure out how to fit the rafters to the ridgepole and walls properly. Phil's leaving in the morning early, leaving Dan and me to figure it out ourselves. *Then* there's the problem of lifting the tent canvas up and over the 10-foot-high ridgepole. I dunno — I feel overwhelmed. It was frustrating wasting such a beautiful day bound to such a technical task. You get so involved you don't want to even eat.

We didn't get the trap in either, because Phil came up and spent the afternoon and evening helping us.

Tomorrow looks like more of the same. The tough thing is that you know if somebody here really knew what they were doing, it would run so much more smoothly.

August 20

Weather: dawned very foggy, so that the plane supposed to carry Phil out at 8 A.M. couldn't find us. Sometime around noon the fog lifted, revealing crystal-clear skies. Later, after Phil left at 2 P.M., a cloud ceiling blew in. Light overcast rest of day. Water very low.

Managed to install the rest of the rafters today, though they didn't line up to my satisfaction or Phil's. Even if they aren't anything a carpenter would be proud of, they should hold the crate together, and I'm no carpenter anyway. Dan put on the plywood sides. Lots stronger now. Will try hoisting and fitting the canvas tent atop the frame tomorrow. I'm less perturbed by the whole business today.

Phil finished his trap before leaving and we installed it. He hurriedly went over instructions for handling fish in the trap, recording data, and keeping records. I'm surprised at how much he expects me to know automatically, or to be able to acquire just by reading instructions. I told him I want to be sure someone who knows what they're doing is here when the heavy runs start, or else he may get something other than what he should from me. Something creative like trying to tag the fish with the shotgun instead of the tag gun.

Dan and I rode up the lake to hike one of the streams at 5 P.M. En route saw at least 35 sockeyes spawning within 75 yards of camp just at the opening of the lake proper. Also, sockeyes are spawning right in front of camp upstream of weir. How am I sure they're spawning? Phil told me so.

Actually, it's fairly obvious. Instead of one milling mass of fish, they are paired up now. In each couple there is a male and a female. (How, I wonder, did any one couple select each other from among so many hundreds? He for the size of his snout, she for her belly bulging with ripe eggs? Gentle nips or nudges?) The male tends to position himself just downstream of the female, at her side. Mostly they just appear to be waiting, but periodically she will turn on her side and flap at the gravel with her powerful tail.

I watched one breeding pair for about 30 minutes. In that time a persistent trout—hoping no doubt to pilfer some eggs—moved in and was driven off at least ten times by the attentive male. Over the next few days this routine will probably be repeated hundreds of times.

We proceeded to the southernmost of the streams entering the east side of the lake (Stream A). Just before reaching it, we saw at least 20 more sockeye in some shallows. No sign of any spawners of any species in the stream, which we ascended for about 1 mile. We walked beyond where I think salmon would get.

August 21

midmorning water level 58.3 centimeters
midmorning water temp. 58 degrees F

Weather: mostly sunny in morning; mostly cloudy afternoon; light rain evening

We got the tent over our frame today. Was easier than we expected—took only about 30–45 minutes. Hardest part was pulling the ridge hole over our extended ridgepole. Later we made a door and steps and pulled the fly over. Things are falling into place, and not all over the place. Our finished product is like the lumber we used: rough-cut. But it'll do.

Sockeyes still spawning in front of us and just up toward the lake. Dan and I went for a ride in the boat early eve. Saw at least 100 sockeye along the east side of the lake in shallow places. Probably many more we missed. We started up a stream we thought led to the little pond Phil had previously sampled from. I think instead we ascended the one shown on the USGS map to the west. Judging by the size of the gravel bars, this should be one of the largest streams feeding into the lake, but now, except for a few tiny pools, it is bone-dry. Its base-flow must actually run below all the gravel. It will be interesting to see if fish spawn in this stream when it rises.

The west side of the lake seems devoid of sockeyes. It falls off too sharply.

We found several sockeye carcasses washed up on shore.

August 22   *9 A.M. water level 61.5 centimeters*

                              9 A.M. water temp. 58 degrees F

Weather: rained the whole previous night, as indicated by water level, which climbed 3.2 cm from day before. Overcast, misting & raining the entire day.

Spent the day in camp doing odds and ends. I worked on bracing the floor in several unsupported spots. We staked out the fly. Dan tightened the cables to the weir anchors. Still need to add some half-inch rope between turnbuckle and first pipe. In afternoon we put a catwalk on the weir. Rather than nailing 2-by-12's together, we've overlapped them. Seems to work.

In the evening, Dan reported there were fish in the trap! The son of a guns got here several days too early for me: I'm still unsure of several procedures and we didn't have a table set up in the trap. Also, we hadn't worked out such basic questions as to where and how to release the fish once through sampling them. No leisure time to read up on it; the fish won't wait. I took a crash course in floy tagging. [The floy tag is a skinny plastic tag, typically two to three inches long, with a number printed on it. The tag is inserted into a fish with a gunlike device that pushes a needle under its dorsal (back) fin; a twisting motion of the tagger's wrist will then lock the tag into place. If the tagger flinches when jabbing the fish with the needle, the placement can be poor and the tag will likely fall out.]

Dan reported a chum and a small (possibly jack) coho. We both got into the trap and in trying to net the fish, somehow, unbelievably, they forced their way through the trap pickets! The smaller fish (probably a coho) disappeared upstream of the weir—our first setback. The chum hung around just outside the pickets and we were able to herd him back in.

We put him in the tub and anesthetized him with the powdered anesthetic drug MS-222. Put him on the measuring board and tried a practice floy tag. The rod would shoot out and the plastic tag would slip to one side without penetrating the fish's skin—didn't seem to work properly. Something missing? Sure enough. Talked to Larry Derby (an experienced "fish monger" on Baranof Island) on the radio at 9 P.M. and asked him a bundle of questions. Found out that a needle has to be attached, through which the rod pushes the tag end. Tried to hide what a dolt I felt like.

I am not at all confident that things will work out once we have a bunch of fish to handle.

August 23   A.M. *water level 66.7 centimeters*
                                      A.M. *water temp. 58 degrees F*

Weather: rain & fog continue; seems to be improving a bit

This has definitely been one of those days when everything seems to be conspiring against you. I currently feel like a nincompoop at best and a complete incompetent at worst, though this may be too soft a judgment. Most of the morning has seen my mood depressed into the nether regions somewhere between panic and despair.

We had 13 fish in the trap this morning—3 chums and 10 cohos. Before going at 'em I talked to Leon in Juneau and managed to get a few questions in about procedures and our setup inside the trap and the floy tagging. Hope I didn't sound too panicked, or they'll be nibbling their fingernails all day long in Juneau wondering if we botched things.

In the trap a bit later we had trouble immediately just in netting the fish and getting them in the tub, for which we still had no table or platform. They each flipped and flopped and put up a terrible fuss. I don't see how we're ever going to keep scale cards dry!!! I got splashed a number of times and I was just recording.

I had found the needle for the gun and practiced first on the 3 chums we had. After once or twice I thought I had the hang of it. The half-teaspoon of MS-222 did not seem to be making the fish very "manageable." Three times out of four that we had them on the measuring board, they'd flop or wriggle free—sometimes to fall into the tub again, sometimes all the way back into the trap. It was frustrating, because we were trying to minimize handling and banging them up. Damn slippery fish! I wanted to sandpaper their slime off so they wouldn't slip out of our hands so easily. Several of them (of the 13 we sampled) bled slightly in the gills, one fairly profusely. (It seemed to recover.)

However, the second coho seemed helpless when we released her from the trap. This was odd because she'd put up a real fight as we handled her. Dan had to clamp her to his chest with all his might to keep her from struggling away. We put everything down for the next 45 minutes and held her upright, moving her gently back and forth, swishing water through her motionless gills. She seemed to be improving, for ever so faintly, her gills began to quiver back into motion. It was like giving CPR to a person. Our hopes rose, but a short while later I noticed her belly-up, dead.

Since this was only our second coho, I figured I'd better call up Juneau and ask about the MS-222, how long the fish can be handled out of water, how long they can stay in the tub with MS-222, etc. I was disturbed by the outcome not just because of the waste but also because she didn't seem heavily drugged when we handled her and yet she then succumbed. Was she in the tub too long? Out of the water too long? Mishandled? Stressed to death?

Dan set up the radio, but when I went to use it the blinking red light did not come on when I tried to transmit. Just when we needed some urgent advice, we're cut off from everyone! I fumbled around for a few minutes with the mike but couldn't get it working. It's not wet and it's plugged in properly. The other alternative is just that the light itself is broken, so that a transmission is going through but no one is answering.

With the rain pelleting us, we went back and finished the rest of the fish. All told, it must've taken 2–3 hours for just 13 fish. At this pace we'll be sampling this fall's run into next summer, and we didn't even take scales.

Sexing the fish was sheer guesswork. Most of them were still quite silvery — didn't seem to have gotten their breeding colors yet. Not a pronounced snout on any of them. Have to find out what to go by in telling the guys from the gals.

Only one of the 10 cohos may have been adipose-clipped, but I wasn't sure. Has the entire adipose been removed or just part of it? At this stage I feel totally unsuited for this line of work. Maybe I'll go into hairdressing. Hope things improve.

Later

Well, things have indeed gone from bad to worse. Found another dead coho a little while ago — #9008 — the one that was bleeding badly at the gills when we released him. Judging from the strong way he swam off, we thought he wasn't hurt that badly. That's 2 mortalities out of 10 cohos in total, or 20% mortalities from our handling alone. At this rate we'll destroy the fishery in this system.

Still can't get radio microphone to transmit.

August 24

midday water level 85.0 centimeters
midday water temp. 58 degrees F

Weather: continuing rain, mist, wind . . . storm? Basically very wretched out. Everything goes to pieces in weather like this. We're still living in our small tents on ground, still cooking outside, still shoving everything under plastic sheets. No time to move into wall-tent.

Well, today an armada of cohos and other allied salmonids arrived. We handled a total of 75 fish in the trap—a long and wet day. Still, things improved considerably over yesterday. *No* mortalities I could see, except for one DOA (a salmon Dead on Arrival at the trap this morning). It looked healthy and showed no wounds. Claustrophobia? Started taking scales today on those fish we felt we could sex.

Many, many more cohos waiting to get into trap. We shut it for night 'cause it's got about 30 fish inside already.

Hope this crappy weather craps out soon and gives us a break. I'd like to move into the warm, dry wall-tent.

Radio mike still inoperative. Didn't sound like anyone got through to anyone else this morning.

August 25   *midday water level 81.7 centimeters*
midday water temp. 57 degrees F

Weather: rained lightly most or all of night. In the morning it seemed as if we would get a reprieve—the fog lifted & rain stopped and a patch or two of faded blue appeared. This lasted 2–3 hours before the rain started again. Still raining now at 8 P.M.

Perhaps 3 dozen sockeye are now spawning right in front of camp just upstream of weir. Have noticed 2–3 dead sockeyes float up against weir, their life energy spent. Others are still alive, but their gills beat feebly and they can no longer resist the current. It's their last gasp. They seem to be falling apart right before our eyes.

Schools of silvers [cohos] continue to climb to the weir. We went through a bunch this morning and then opened the trap again to let 'er fill. Maybe 20–30 inside now and more just below weir.

Good reception on radio this morning. Heard all of southeast Alaska but no one could hear me. Leon Shaul tried reaching us; didn't get my reply. Opened mike and looked at it. Everything looks OK. Not wet. Am I missing something obvious?

Realized today I might've mistaken steelhead/rainbow trout for pinks. Will have to remember to count rays on anal fin tomorrow. One of the little gals I handled (pink?) laid eggs on me when I grabbed her in the tub, confirming that I really do have a way with women. Recent experiences with human females had left me in doubt.

Still losing too many floy tags, even when I think I've inserted the needle, compressed the lever, and twisted properly. Don't know whether it's me, the fish, or the gun. Also, sometimes it jams and sometimes tags get crossed up. I can tell whether or not it's a good tag job by how deeply the tag is buried when I withdraw the needle.

Messing with these fish in August chills me. I can hardly wait for November!

August 26   A.M. *water level 80.0 centimeters*
P.M. *water level 100.0 centimeters*
(up to 104 centimeters at dusk!)
A.M. *water temp. 57 degrees F*

Weather: cloudy & spitting rain in morning; bucketfuls of rain in afternoon; thus the rapid rise in water level—20 cm. over 5 or 6 hours

The cohos continued their assault on our fortress today, but we knocked 'em off one by one. Our procedure has really improved—we know exactly where to stand, where to place pencils, forceps, tag gun, how to grip fish, which way to place them on measuring board, where to pluck off scales, and so on. I feel much better about what we're doing. Of course I still don't know whether we're even doing things right! But we're out of contact with civilization (still) and simply have to wing (or fin) it.

Dan tried the wet suit on for our fish handling today. It may be superior to rain gear once the water and air temp. drops. The chief disadvantage is getting it on and off—it's a real *commitment*. You have to be sure you've done your doo-doo first.

Dan found one of yesterday's tagged fish—#9133—dead under our boat today. Fortunately there were no next of kin to notify, for our radio still doesn't transmit.

It's 10:30 P.M. now and raining harder than ever. The water is already up 'n over our table in the trap. Don't know what we'll do tomorrow: it's simply jumping with fish.

*

Dear Folks,

For the first time in a week or two I'm, 1) sitting down; and 2) feeling the sun in my face. I've been more than earning my keep here in the bush. It has been extremely hectic getting this research operation all set up before the heavy rains, higher waters, and spawning coho salmon inundate us. It rains all the time here, almost on a daily schedule, just more or less of it. I've been frequently working to 11 P.M. nonstop all day. The two major things we've had to build are a weir and a wall-tent platform and frame.

A weir is a fence across a stream that controls what can move up the stream. Ours consists of a series of tripods made of four-by-six lumber. The tripods support "channels" and "pickets." We have eighteen tripods in our weir. The pickets are hollow metal rods (electrical conduit), and these are what block the passage of fish of a particular size. We capture the fish in a trap into which they swim. We then count them, check them for marks and scars, etc. The data obtained from this field research are then used in management of the commercial fishery in ways I don't yet fully understand.

Our wall-tent is a fourteen-by-sixteen-foot structure, about ten and a half feet high at the peak. It is made of white, heavy canvas and rests on two-by-fours and plywood. Inside are shelves, bunks, a huge table, and stools. We're making it pretty cozy now. We had to construct it from scratch, including the selection of a site.

It took Dan Hutchins and me about three times as long as it should have; doing something, undoing something when we'd screwed up, then redoing it. The boss biologist, who was around for a couple of days, had his doubts about my competence! For example, we had just set up four tree stumps to use for supports to lift the floor frame off the ground, and then laid on four two-by-sixes that outlined the floor frame. I very meticulously leveled each side up and then called to Phil, who was working at something else, to come look at it. What he saw looked like a trapezoid. I was concentrating so much on leveling everything that I had forgotten all about making it square.

I'd also forgotten how just one poor fit in a frame can be so insidiously compounded throughout the whole structure. Getting the angles right on the rafters was particularly knotty business. We had arguments about just how tightly they had to fit. Indeed, communicating your ideas or your objections to what you thought someone else's ideas were was half the trouble. It was remarkable that after every day of scraping around there was any net progress at all! Yet there always was. I'd forgotten how utterly absorbing work like that can be. Stopping to eat is only a bother. We wouldn't quit until the darkness made it impossible to continue.

I guess the last time I ever really did much of this sort of construction carpentry was around the house with you, Dad, and then I simply pounded nails, mixed cement, and daydreamed. I never paid much attention to the calculations and decisions. Then later on, I avoided such work not because I detested it, but because I didn't like looking like an inept boob in front of other people. (Nobody does!) Too many people have ridiculed my "lack of common sense," so I avoided situations where I would have revealed ignorance, but that would've taught me something all the same.

Another embarrassing incident occurred over siphoning gas out of a barrel with a plastic tube. I'd always thought you get a siphon going by first sucking with your mouth and filling the tube with the fluid. But when I tried this with the tube Phil had gotten us, which was thick and about eight feet long, there was no way you could suck hard enough to get a siphon action started. My partner actually got several mouthfuls of gas trying! He cut the tube in half and then it worked, although not easily.

Well, the boss came back and we asked why he'd sent such a thick, long tube that it was almost useless for siphoning. We thought we'd finally caught him doing something stupid! Wishful thinking. It was only then that I discovered you fill the tube simply by lowering it into the gas and then capping the end with your thumb. I was furious with myself for not being able to figure out something so simple and obvious. You see, I *do* lack common sense quite often, and I don't like it displayed to myself or to other people! I later heard that the siphon story was repeated back at the office in Juneau with many laughs and doubts expressed as to our competence.

Oh well, I *am* learning things the hard way, and overall, I think I'm making a favorable impression.

The cohos started running upstream this week with a spate of bad weather we've had. Dan and I managed to figure out how to do things with no one else around to tell us how, while we were out of radio contact for four days.

I was frantic the morning the first ten cohos appeared in our trap. I was also a bit furious because I'd been assured one of the biologists would come out to show me everything once the fish began running. You have to anesthetize the fish to be able to measure and tag them and take scale samples. If you hit them with too much anesthetic you can injure or kill them; too little, and they're ten to fifteen pounds of fighting fury and can injure or kill themselves while thrashing around. The biggest cohos are well over two feet long. Well, we killed the second fish we handled.

I threw up my arms in dismay and disgust and tried to contact Juneau for immediate advice. And then, just when I needed it most, the radio microphone went on the blink. I was positive the boss would think it was because we had let it get wet. It was a black, black day. I had to fend off a feeling of total despair and failure. We processed ten fish, but two of them died at our hands. It took us three hours, and I could see dozens more fish behind the weir waiting to go upstream. The thought that there would be days when a hundred or more fish would deluge us boggled my mind.

Somehow I managed to keep from going to pieces and did some creative thinking at the same time. I managed to come up with some better ideas for the next day. By the evening I sensed I'd weathered the crisis, and felt peace of mind again. One of the biologists just came in yesterday, and he seems pleased with the results of our sink-or-swim efforts. Things should go more smoothly now.

As I mentioned during our last phone talk from Juneau before I left, there are many tools and machines to know how to use and maintain: a two-way radio and associated 12-volt battery, portable generator, chain saw, outboard motor, twelve-gauge shotgun, oil-burning heating stove, lanterns, and Coleman cooking stoves. There is a special lubricant for the chain saw, a special fuel mix for the outboard motor, and a separate one for the chain saw, a special tool for this, a special oil for that, and on and on. If I don't have common sense after this . . . I'm uncommonly dumb!

This place is lonely and wild. The occasional floatplane that you hear but do not see is the only other intrusion of the human race. Each morning we turn on our radio and listen in to the goings-on of commercial fisheries research people all over southeast Alaska, across hundreds of miles of rugged mountains and fjords. It's neat to hear those disembodied voices crackle out of the radio set, to think of the invisible electromagnetic waves permeating the air, and the ability of the antenna to snatch them out of it. I picture other Fish and

Game employees huddled over their sets communicating, in spite of the rain, the fog, the mountains, the sea, and the distance that divides us. Most of these people I'll never even meet, but I know their radio voices. One woman at the Chilkoot weir has a particularly cheerful voice. It's something to fantasize about.

Last week we never saw the sun once. Hell, it got to the point where a mere drizzle was good weather, uplifting our soggy spirits. The wall-tent at least is dry, and now that we have installed an oil stove, it will be warm as well, as the weather worsens.

The forest here is timeless and ancient. It is composed almost exclusively of two great trees: western hemlock, which is closely related to the eastern hemlock, and Sitka spruce. The largest spruces would take maybe four people with arms extended to circle them. They must be over five hundred years old. They were already of respectable age and size even when the only peoples in this land had red skin, and they will probably still be standing a century or more after we have all perished and left this world for the next.

I do feel lonesome out here, but it's not a terrible thing. I often feel lonesome just thinking about the destiny of each and every one of us anyway. It's just that here the solitude amplifies your feelings and emotions. Right now for example, I miss you both very much, and I lament being so far from home for so long. But if I were home of course, unavoidably, I would take you for granted. That "absence makes the heart grow fonder" is one of life's greatest truisms, and one of its greatest ironies as well. You don't know what you've got 'til it's gone, even when you know better.

Well, the westering sun and rising tide tell me it's time to get on with things. I'll send this out with the next plane. One day, in several months, another plane will carry me out into the wide world again; then it won't be long until we reunite!

Love,
Leon

*

August 30

Weather: overcast & rainy

With the arrival of Detlef Büttner and Leon Shaul over the weekend, I couldn't bring myself to keep up with my notes. Sorry about that, Daily Log. Shaul departed this morning with Dan Hutchins, and solitude returned today.

Their flight out was not a little harrowing, even for us observers on the ground. Shaul thought he could skimp and save the project money by ordering a smaller Cessna 180 instead of a more expensive full-sized Beaver. When Ken the pilot pulled up, his face did not wear the jovial expression it usually does. Rather, it registered dismay at the mound of gear Leon hoped to fit in. "All that?" he frowned.

Well, it wouldn't *all* stuff in, but they packed it so heavy the plane seemed to sink lower in the water—and *that* certainly can't be a good sign. As they motored to the far end of the lake I caught one last glimpse of Shaul's face pressed against the window, a helpless prisoner now. Judging from his grim expression, I think he was already wondering if he'd signed his own death warrant!

We watched anxiously as Ken throttled it, and the valley boomed with an earsplitting blare as the plane shot forward and strained to lift off. It had gone half the length of the lake before it slowly cleared itself of the dragging water. At that moment, inexplicably, the pilot cut back and the floats splashed down again. Had they forgotten something? I asked myself. But no, apparently Ken decided there wasn't enough distance left to clear the tall trees at the lake's other end.

They circled back toward the far edge. But this time, still pointed the opposite direction, Ken accelerated even before reaching the corner, and they swept around in a wide 180-degree curve, building up velocity. The floats struggled free of the water earlier and the plane slowly climbed 10, 20, 30 feet and more. I was amazed at how slowly; this plane wasn't meant for a load this heavy. At the end of the lake it soared over the topmost snags of the 150-foot trees so closely that the branches swayed in the backwash. We finally let our breath go.

Ten minutes later we saw it again, ascending in large circles, slowly gaining the altitude necessary for the flight back to Juneau. Leon told me afterward that normally cheerful Ken didn't say a word till about halfway back. By the time they landed in Juneau, he was merry and whistling again. Nevertheless, even though he is not one to reprimand, Ken said to Leon: "Never again!" Shaul agreed 100 percent!

We have now seen 2 floy-tagged fish that are covered with a fungus. Shaul thinks we may not be dosing the fish heavily enough, thus having to handle them severely. We are experimenting with ways to minimize handling and trauma.

Today we found an *untagged* coho above weir. Don't know how it got there. Was in bad shape. We caught and examined it. Had blood on belly, a ragged adipose, and circular spots of what appeared to be a fungus. Believe it later died.

August 31

P.M. water level 115 centimeters
P.M. water temp. 54 degrees F

Weather: drizzle and rain all day

This morning we had perhaps 100 cohos in the trap. However, the water level was so high we simply could not stand on the stream bottom and work, as we always have before. So we spent most of the day preparing a new platform and table arrangement that will allow us to stand several feet off the stream bottom and still reach fish in the trap.

We discovered 3 fish today, all with our floy tags (#9023, 9089, 9090) that were dead or nearly so and covered with large patches of fungus (mold?) especially concentrated just in front of the tail, suggesting that the fungus has developed where the fish was gripped. This is beginning to really concern us. If we have now seen a total of 4 fish with this condition, how many more has it affected that we haven't seen? Is it due to our handling? Can it be curbed?

I neglected to note previously that on August 28, Detlef and I walked to tidewater. We saw hundreds of spawning chums (200–300?) and hundreds, if not thousands, of spawning pinks. Perhaps 300 cohos were noted within several hundred yards of the weir; none below that. No live sockeyes observed.

Just as we happened upon the tidal meadow at the stream's mouth, we saw a brown bear ambling toward us about 100 yards away along the beach. We stopped dead in our tracks. We were downwind of it, so presumably it couldn't sniff us. Somehow it detected us anyway, for within 30 seconds of our sighting it, it stood up on 2 legs, dropped down, and dove for the cover of the nearby woods.

September

September 1

noon water level 96 centimeters
8 P.M. water level 146 centimeters
noon water temp. 52.5 degrees F

Weather: soft drizzle most of night & morning; full-fledged storm in afternoon, accounting for the 50-cm. jump in water level in several hours

We tested out our new setup for working in higher waters today (an elevated platform to stand and place tub and measuring board on). Although it's more cramped and movement is inhibited, it should work out.

This afternoon gusts and driving rains battered us. By evening, the water level had risen an astonishing 50+ centimeters over what it was at noon, all the way up to and barely over the highest row of channel, a mere 1 foot from the top of the pickets. (I thought this wasn't due till October! Then again neither were 300 cohos in one week.) We set to work securing the trap and stringing chicken wire across about half the length of the weir. We also ran vinyl-coated wire from the end of the weir on the camp side up the natural levee there to nearly the edge of the woods. The water was within 1 foot of topping the levee. It's now 2 A.M. (Sept. 2) and the waters may have crested, although sporadic blasts of rain still pummel the tent roof.

Cohos were jumping in the trap and several leaps we saw nearly cleared the 10-foot vertical pickets. It seems possible that we may have lost a few.

September 2   *8 A.M. water level 137 centimeters*
                        8 P.M. water level 109 centimeters
                        8 P.M. water temp. 52 degrees F

Weather: improved a lot. Why, it only rained intermittently throughout the day, instead of continually! Actually, we saw some sun too. Beautiful, uplifting. Brought out the bugs . . .

Detlef found another fungus-covered coho, #9049 (from Dan's and my second day of tagging—Aug. 24), backed up to the weir and near death. He put it to sleep and retrieved the floy tag. We are hoping our new handling procedures (more MS-222, and measuring, tagging, and taking scales while fish are in the tub), as well as floy-tagging only about half the fish, will cut down on this problem.

September 3   *noon water level 89 centimeters*
                        noon water temp. 51.5 degrees F

Weather: absolutely glorious for a welcome change. Sunny & bright in morning; high thin clouds afternoon.

We ran through a number of cohos today (51 total), moving much more quickly than the previous 2 days because of lower water (making it easier to maneuver when netting the fish), warmer weather (the better for hands to operate more efficiently), and a more rapid procedure.

We finished all our chores by 3:30 and at 4 P.M. went for a hike up the mountain behind camp (south of the lake—el. 2,329 feet on the USGS topo). Our approach route was via the southernmost of the three streams on the eastern side of the lake. We followed it to about the limit of salmon ascent but saw no cohos. Did see one sockeye near outlet of stream into lake that we inadvertently chased upstream.

Above timberline we enjoyed the extensive views, sunshine, and openness. Found where all the deer have been hiding. Depending on how many sightings were recounts, we saw between 10–20 Sitka black-tailed deer (a subspecies of the mule deer). Got back just as darkness descended. An altogether productive, satisfying day.

September 5   *10 A.M. water level 73.5 centimeters*
8 P.M. water level 89 centimeters
8 P.M. water temp. 54 degrees F

Weather: overcast, blustery & raining much of day

Today we did chores around camp, like tinkering with the old Coleman stove and the new one, placing sandbags on the upstream side of all the pickets in the weir, and working on a walkway through the mud.

Detlef went fishing downstream in the evening. At a large pool about 250 yards below the weir he observed "more than a hundred" cohos where he and I had seen large numbers on our walk to tidewater a week ago.

Two or three dozen sockeyes continue to spawn right in front of camp. Five or ten a day are now washing up against the weir, dead or nearly so. Some are already quite decomposed and absolutely putrid. The worst actually break in half as we try to lob them over the weir—these are the "creamers."

I'm getting the scale samples from those that are not too rotten. Because they are tinier and more firmly attached than coho scales, sockeye scales are much harder to yank off with the forceps. Especially our *blunt* forceps. Sometimes the stench is so nauseating we must hold our breath, then dash away to gasp at fresh air.

September 6   *3 P.M. water level 126 centimeters*
8 P.M. water level 145 centimeters
3 P.M. water temp. 52 degrees F

Weather: stormy

Today seemed like a repeat performance of our flood just 5 days ago. We were battered with wind and rain much of the day and lo! the waters rose in unison.

These high waters are troublesome because we can't get at the fish in the trap even with our new standing arrangement. Right now we stand and have the tub on a plywood platform 3 feet above the stream bottom inside the trap. The fish all congregate under the platform when we try to net them. If the water is no higher than about 110 centimeters this is no problem. Above that, we can't stand on the stream bottom in our chest waders without filling up with water. If the waters are going to consistently rise this high, we'll have to devise something new.

I saw 5 large ducks float down the river below the weir tonight.

Continuing to retrieve sockeye carcasses and trying to yank the scales out of them. Blunt forceps, pelting rain, and smelly, slimy carcasses can make life miserable. Many of my scales may be upside down and torn. I have to yank so hard I can't tell whether or not they flip over. Also, the lateral line is very obscure on many of these sockeyes.

We heard several gunshots from the mountain above us this afternoon. At least they sounded like gunshots. Very strange considering the incredibly inclement weather. Was it thunder? (Unusual for the Northwest.)

September 7

2 P.M. water level 121 centimeters

2 P.M. water temp. 50.5 degrees F

Weather: mixed periods of rain and unrain. A rather bright day, even with all the rain.

We worked all afternoon until dusk processing fish. Cleared the trap of 115 cohos, almost double our previous daily high. Also got scales from 14 sockeyes washing up dead or nearly so against the weir. A tough day for the sockeyes I guess.

One fish pulled off a most amazing stunt—and so thwarted our efforts to keep orderly records. While we were starting to load the tub with another batch of fish, it jumped (as cohos will do) at the pickets on the upstream side of the trap—and became lodged 3 feet above water between the corner pole and a picket! Detlef rushed over toward it, and in his hasty efforts to extract it, it got out of the trap (upstream of weir) without our seeing whether it was marked or unmarked. This fish must've been an escape artist in its former life.

Using more MS-222 seems to be the way to go. Though the fish do take longer to recover, they all seem to. Hope this cures the fungus problem.

September 9   10 A.M. water level 79 centimeters
                                 10 A.M. water temp. 50 degrees F

Weather: brilliant & sunny morn. 80% cloud cover (mostly cumulus) afternoon.

As the day dawned crisp and clean, we decided early to polish off our daily chores and head for the high country as soon as possible. We ran through 18 cohos and 5 chums in the trap quickly. Our procedures are now becoming polished and "professional." We are definitely faster and, I hope, less hard on the fish. We don't even lift them entirely out of the water, only far enough to insert a tag under the dorsal fin and pluck several scales off.

Yesterday I closed off the space in the trap beneath our standing and tub platform. Used the diving mask and wetsuit to attach hardware cloth with wire underwater. This will make it much easier to net fish, especially in higher water.

Our hike today was good. We climbed the unnamed 2,635-foot mountain to the northwest of Ford Arm Lake. Got views of the 2 other large unnamed lakes in the vicinity (els. 920 feet and 423 feet); saw about 20 deer and 6 ptarmigan.

Today we reestablished radio contact with Outside for the first time in a week. At first I thought bad weather throughout the region was impeding communication; but after things improved and we still heard very little on the set and could reach no one, I suspected the radio itself. The hydrometer showed the battery to be still well within the "good" range, but after I recharged it anyway, we finally got through to Juneau. Earlier when Leon tried to contact us and I replied, he didn't receive our transmission, so perhaps the battery was weak, despite the high hydrometer reading.

September 10   2 P.M. water level 73 centimeters
                                 2 P.M. water temp. 50.5 degrees F

Weather: wild & windy; blew most of the day and drizzled most of afternoon

The day began auspiciously with the sighting of a grizzly bear on the opposite stream bank, mere yards from the weir, not to mention mere yards (about 25) from where I stood at the trap. I caught sight of it when I heard something walking through the brush. It was moving *away* from me, so it had been even closer to this unsuspecting *Homo sapiens*. I watched it munch on a salmon for a few minutes before I called Detlef to come and look. I distinctly heard the crunching of fish bones in powerful bear jaws—the sort of sound that stays with you.

While I watched the bear, a flock of about 20 Canada geese flew overhead, honking loudly and in customary V-formation. Autumn is on its way.

There were only a few fish in the trap, not surprising considering the low water level. The day's sum total consisted of just 3 chums.

I thought the radio was behaving itself again but I discovered otherwise today. In talking to Leon in Juneau this morning our signal faded out. Don't know why; the battery is charged so high it nearly sends the hydrometer into orbit. Each cell has a reading of about 1,300 (the maximum on the scale). Will hope things improve Monday. We have a grocery list we want to relay.

In the afternoon we walked the outlet stream to tidewater. There are still many spawning pinks and chums, but they looked much less fresh and there are many more dead fish now, eyes picked out by the birds, some chopped in half, presumably by some bear. Rough estimates are 200–400 chums and 1,000–2,000 pinks. At least half the pinks occur in the final 300–400 yards of the stream, just before it heads through a gap and empties into the ocean. Here there is only one stream channel with cobble-sized stones and a moderate current. The chums are spread more evenly throughout the distance from weir to sea.

The tide was up, inundating much of the meadow at the outlet of the stream emptying into Ford Arm. Half a dozen eagles and many gulls and ravens were enjoying their own version of the Juneau Salmon Derby. The air reverberated with the eagles' defiant shrieks, the gulls' raucous cries, and the hoarse croaks of the ravens. A group of about 10 harbor seals lay just offshore. Poking their heads up to peer silently at us, they looked like little whiskered monks. Two actually shot past us upstream a short distance, enabled by the high tide.

After a lifetime of feasting on smaller fish and other organisms, these salmon are now themselves the main course in this annual feast for the benefit of still other birds and beasts. Just paying their dues to the ecological community.

We also saw an estimated 200–400 cohos all massed in one 40–50-yard stretch of the stream about 250 yards below the weir. The water is 2–4 feet deep in this area and flows very gently, although I would not quite call it a "pool." They seem to be holding in this spot, waiting for higher water to move upstream.

We returned to find a bear—probably the same from the morning—right beside the far end of the weir from camp. It was munching on salmon. (What else?) Though it became aware of our presence, it did not flee, but alternately looked toward us and went about its business. At one point it began messing with our final section of pickets leading to the bank from the last tripod. It moved some rocks, a sandbag or two, and some chicken wire out of the way, and looked to be digging for something. I didn't like the way it was interfering with our facilities. I hope we are not witnessing a "problem bear" in the making . . . stay tuned!

September 11   *9 A.M. water level 74.5 centimeters*
                                 9 A.M. water temp. 49 degrees F

Weather: light winds & rain morning; partly cloudy afternoon

Yes, we definitely have the makings of a problem bear on our hands. Between the noise of our house mouse scampering all over our food and the bear and fish banging around the pickets last night, I had a hard time getting to sleep. At 1:30 A.M. I got up and went out. There he (she?) sat, just 15 feet downstream of the weir, staring at me. I insulted him loudly several times, to no avail. I tried in German once, but that didn't work either, so back to bed.

In the morning, I step out the door and whoahh! he's right in the garbage bags, 20 yards from the wall-tent toward the weir. Now he's getting too close to home for comfort, so I threw several things and shouted. I guess it would be like a gnat shouting at me; anyway, it had the same effect. He walked away slowly, as if I wasn't the cause of his leaving at all.

Later in the day we saw a bear halfway up the lake that looked like our visitor. Maybe he'll give us a break. Maybe not.

In the evening we walked up and down the two inlet streams closest to camp on the east side of the lake. We saw no sign of any salmon of any species in either of the two. The temperature of the southernmost was 48 degrees F. Tomorrow we will explore the other two inlet streams, including the one draining the small unnamed pond.

Henceforth in this log, for the sake of both brevity and clarity, I will christen each of the 4 inlet streams with 4 original designations contrived especially for this research. Proceeding from camp along the east side of Ford Arm Lake, we first reach Stream A, followed by streams B, C, and D. Sometimes my raw creativity astonishes me.

September 12   *10 A.M. water level 72.5 centimeters*
                                          8 P.M. water level 71 centimeters
                                          10 A.M. water temp. 51 degrees F

Weather: warm & partly sunny, yet another wonderful day. We're cheating Mother Nature. When will she strike back?

Cohos still appear to be waiting downstream—saw several small groups venture up to the weir and check it over, but none really entered trap.

This afternoon we again scouted out inlet streams. Stream D had a single female sockeye about 50 yards above the outlet. Judging by her spent appearance, she had already spawned.

After exploring Stream D, we took a compass bearing and plunged into deep woods aiming for the nameless pond northeast of Ford Arm Lake. We found it without much trouble. The pond is surrounded by extensive horsetail-dominated marshes. As we approached the edge, it felt like walking atop a springy mat or sponge of peat. I was leery of breaking through. I suppose the whole open area, devoid of all but spindly trees (coastal variety of lodgepole pine), would qualify as a bog or muskeg.

The outlet of the pond is very obscure. At last we found it from a maze of incised channels and followed it to the lake. It is shorter than I thought it would be. No sign of cohos. Water temp. in the marshy flats just before entry into the lake was 51 degrees F.

Detlef saw what was either a muskrat, mink, or small otter just where Stream C drains the pond. The 2 of us saw 2 ducks on the pond (species unknown) and 5 other water birds on the lake (ID uncertain, but I think they were grebes).

Another bear episode today. I opened the door this morning to be greeted by a very dark, almost black, grizzly 10–15 yards away, right by our fire pit. It gave a snort and bolted into the brush. I'm almost certain that this is a different bear from the one we saw yesterday morning. I guess the news is spreading. Our garbage was again raided. Tomorrow I will put it into a new bag and hoist it over a tree limb. Probably should have done so already.

This afternoon when I went to use the chain saw, I discovered the chain-saw fuel container was missing. Detlef walked immediately over to a spot where he thought he'd heard a bear last evening. Sure enough, there it was, a little chewed on, but intact. Only the fuel was missing! Undoubtedly our thieving friend considered that brew a real treat. Has more of a kick than water.

This evening we noticed that one large plastic bowl and one plastic glass left outside to dry, as well as one of our plastic washbasins, all had tooth-holes in them. We didn't find it entertaining. I am beginning to fret that even the interior of the wall-tent—our last sanctuary—is not inviolate to these marauders.

September 13

11 A.M. water level 69 centimeters
11 A.M. water temp. 52 degrees F

Weather: clear night and early morning, but began to cloud over by mid-morn & by nightfall was heavy overcast & misting

Not much to report. A break from bear hassles—there were none to be seen this morn. Our "mousies" were at it again last night though, driving us batty with their incessant scampering and nibbling. Leaning on one arm in my bunk, I spotted the furry little bandits in the beam of my flashlight—two of them—scampering with impunity among the boxes and bags of food scattered all across our table. In the morning they had left their telltale sign: plastic bags and cardboard boxes with holes nibbled through them, as well as trails of their round, dark little calling cards. (The previous night Detlef was actually nipped or scratched on the back of his neck by one of these little stinkers. Tonight he will try to catch them. I will be his sidekick in this dubious endeavor.)

No fish again today, presumably because of low water that prevails.

Managed to contact Juneau and talk to Phil this afternoon and relay "most" of our grocery list to him. Was again unable to reach Juneau this morning. Radio would fade out after awhile, so that we had to keep turning it up to hear other stations, until the static drowns out voices altogether.

We are running low on key food items. Out of peanut butter, almost out of cheese, small amount of powdered milk left, fresh bread gone, no meat, no fresh veggies, no juices, one dozen eggs left, a few potatoes, and lots of boring canned goods. Green beans for breakfast anyone? If we're lucky tonight, we may get mouse stew.

Went for a hike late afternoon up the ridge leading to peak el. 3,205 feet. Saw no cohos in Stream A. Saw 2 deer above timberline. Continued along ridge until whited-out. Had to race the darkness on our descent. We slipped and slid like two carefree, careless fools down some very steep, slick, grassy bluffs. On one Detlef actually did a complete somersault (accidentally) and by the grace of God landed atop a ledge, still on his feet like a cat. That boy is agile! We're both lucky our knees and ankles are still intact.

September 14

2 P.M. water level 154 centimeters
7 P.M. water level 133 centimeters
7 P.M. water temp. 50 degrees F

Weather: torrential downpour half of night into morning caused water level to jump 85 cm. in under 10 hours. Later, rain let up & mist descended.

Well, the fish came up today on cue. This morning I could see dozens of silvery blue, blunt snouts probing between the pickets. We kept the trap closed through the morning however, for we feared the water would rise so high as to make working in it impossible, as well as risk losing some or all of the fish in the trap. The water level crested in early afternoon as the rains abated, so we were able to process some fish in the evening (worked 'til we couldn't see). In just 3 minutes with only one picket lifted, nearly 60 fish piled into the trap.

There will be many more fish to do tomorrow.

The radio seemed to work better today. Contacted Politofski Lake and Juneau A.M.; Politofski again tonight.

No sign of our bear friends today.

September 15   *2 P.M. water level 94 centimeters*
                                  2 P.M. water temp. 50 degrees F

Weather: foggy & socked in all day; windless and quiet

Well, foiled again. Last night just after we'd processed 47 fish we decided to shut the trap because there were so many cohos we thought it would not be conducive to their well-being to have a trap full of them whipping each other up into a frenzy. Since it had taken all of 3 minutes for 50 of them to enter the trap last night, we reasoned we could just open it in the morning and quickly reach our quota.

But the waters retreated and so did the cohos. I suppose they might have backed off even if they had been in the trap. It's interesting that the water is now much higher than it was when significant numbers of cohos started running on Dan and me, and yet now they retreat. I guess this demonstrates that it's not the absolute water level that sets them off, but rising waters, at whatever level.

Saw a very dark grizzly again today, probably the same one I saw several mornings ago right in camp. It was gathering and eating dead salmon on the bank at the far end of the weir. Very enjoyable to watch (we were standing halfway across the 60-yard weir). It's gotten to the point where I really like having the bears around so close; they are so powerful, so legendary, and so much a part of the ecology of this coast. So far none has acted at all threatening to us. Let's hope it stays that way. We are no longer even that frightened at night at the thought of them lurking so close in the darkness. Still, I must say I don't feel as comfortable about taking a piss outside at night here as I do in my bathroom at home.

September 16   *1 P.M. water level 79 centimeters*
                                  1 P.M. water temp. 51 degrees F

Weather: foggy & still, only modest rainfall

A very uneventful day in the timeless rain forest. Only a few fish in the trap. I walked downstream and found hundreds still holing up in the shallow pool 250 yards below weir in which we've observed them before. It occurred to me that, to them, our weir is probably like any natural obstacle to their migration, which is why they don't bother to come up when the water's dropping. As it rises, however, instinct or something tells them that there's now a better chance of their getting over the obstacle because water may be flowing over it. Anyway, small groups of cohos could be seen reconnoitering the weir vicinity.

We have at least 2 mice thieving from us at night. Last night I got so irritated with their scurrying and nibbling and our unsuccessful attempts to catch or kill them that I slept poorly.

September 17

11 *A.M. water level 74 centimeters*
11 *A.M. water temp. 51 degrees F.*

Weather: clear, sunny & warm

For several nights Detlef has been pitting his skills as a hunter and stalker against the wily mousies. Within 20 minutes of blowing out the lantern we begin hearing the persistent gnawing of tiny rodent incisors that tells us these little raiders have begun their nightly depredations. While I shone the flashlight on one or both marauders from my bunk, Detlef would drop out of the lower bunk in his underwear and creep over to the table as stealthily as a lynx. There his unsuspecting prey would be helping itself to some tasty morsel at our expense.

Somehow, just as Detlef was about to swoop down on them, the little rascals always managed to save their scrawny hides. Away they would bolt, darting behind a can of jelly or a box of Special K, until they disappeared in the darkness and tabletop debris. After several futile stalks, Detlef discovered precisely where they were getting onto the table—they scampered up and down one of the 2-by-4 wall studs and onto the table through a gap in the poor fit.

The next night I joined the hunting party. As soon as we heard the whispering of whiskers on the table, we both lowered ourselves to the floor silently and tiptoed to our predetermined positions. Detlef posted himself under the table with a specially made cardboard box, while I went in pursuit of micemeat. Catching the little squirt in my flashlight beam, I chased him over toward his escape hatch. Down he went, no doubt thinking he'd outwitted us once again. Down he went, right into Detlef's box! "I got him! I got him!" shouted

Detlef with glee, and he tilted the box so I could look in to see our prisoner. Seizing its last chance, out hopped the mousie right through our flailing hands, onto the floor and out the door. And we were stumped chumps again.

Last night we set out to restore the wounded pride of the human inhabitants of this woebegone camp. This time Detlef used a plastic zip-lock bag, with which he covered up the slit from beneath. Once again I pursued the mouse down the hole—and right into the bag. This time we had him. Before he could bite his way out, we poured him into a glass jar to await his fate at dawn.

When we awoke and I realized all that separated us from blue skies was some ground fog, I knew we had to go for another hike in the high country. We ate breakfast and cleared the trap of fish (3 chums plus 1 coho) in short order and we were off: Detlef, me, and the marauding mouseketeer that we spent half of last night trying to capture. After discussing various ways of torturing mice, pity overtook us and we merely sent this offender into exile. We released him in the muskeg near the little nameless pond. We may still have others to deal with.

It was an incredible day of ups and downs, and for more than just elevation gains and losses. We climbed 3 mountains southwest of our lake, all nameless, els. 3,205 feet, 2,817 feet, and 2,329 feet. This involved probably 4,500 feet of vertical relief as well as about 15 miles hiking cross-country without the benefit of trails (well, trails made by humans, anyway). At the moment my knees are shot.

The views were stunning. In the early afternoon, puffy clouds and rising mists created continually changing scenery. Later a fog settled over the ocean into which the sun sank as we descended.

We saw about 18 deer, including one 8-point buck that we nearly stepped on an instant after I uttered: "Isn't this lush habitat!" while thinking of how good it would be for deer. We also saw about 20 ptarmigan in one group of 17 and another of 3. One flock of 12 ducks (mergansers) on the lake too.

The climax of the day came when we stepped atop peak el. 2,329 feet and gazed straight down on Ford Arm with fog and luminous clouds suspended above and around in a display of dazzling beauty. I, of course, had run out of film and cursed my lot. Just before Detlef was about to snap a picture, the last on his roll, a handsome young buck strutted into view 20 yards in front of us and virtually *posed* before the breathtaking scene. Detlef got this incredible shot, one that could easily do the cover of *National Wildlife* proud. Moments later, in rewinding his film, it ripped, placing this shot of award-winning potential in jeopardy. Now we both cursed. Later yet, Detlef slipped in a stream and got the inside of his camera wet. Yes, it was a day of high highs and low lows.

September 18

2 *P.M. water level 71 centimeters*
2 *P.M. water temp. 52 degrees F*

Weather: foggy most of morning; cleared midday; was bright and sunny 'til evening, when a cloud ceiling closed in from the west

Spent the morning recovering from yesterday's endeavors.

One of our bears made an appearance this morning. As I opened the door, he ambled up our walkway by our fuel barrels 30 yards from cabin toward stream. He then lay down, yawned, and scratched his nose. He looked more at home in our camp than we are, and in a sense he is, I reckon. He's a permanent resident—we're the visitors.

In the afternoon we walked up each of the inlet streams. No sign of coho spawning activity in any of them. Water level was relatively low, as would be expected. Ascended Stream B, the longest and largest tributary of the lake, about 2 miles to where its gradient steepened substantially in a small gorge. This looked like it might be the limit of salmon movement.

I have a persistent ear infection that is beginning to concern me. Last week it came on pretty painfully in my left ear. It abated, but has now returned, accompanied by the same in my right ear; can feel fluid pressing tight against the drums.

September 20

5 *P.M. water level 67 centimeters*
5 *P.M. water temp. 54 degrees F*

Weather: fog & drizzle A.M.; lifted in P.M. Lovely evening with sun glistening on wet leaves.

A quiet, uneventful day in the woods. The food plane didn't come; it's now been 3½ weeks since the last food drop. Breakfast was pancakes, lunch was pancakes, dinner was fish. I'm stuffed right now. Who can complain?

*

September 20, 1982
Monday

Dear Folks,

Several weeks ago my first partner Dan Hutchins left Ford Arm to work at another lake a couple of hundred miles south on Prince of Wales Island. On the misty morning he left by floatplane, he came over and shook my hand and said he'd enjoyed working with me and was sorry he couldn't have stayed on. I felt genuine warmth toward him, but also a little relieved at his departure. I think three months alone together would be too much of a strain. But I would probably say that about most people.

Given what I learned about Dan, it would embarrass me terribly if he ever discovered some of the wild conjectures we made about him initially. Fortunately for me, everybody's first impressions were off; you couldn't judge this book by its cover, at least not all of its pages.

In a nutshell, Dan is very "different," perhaps like an old cowboy or Indian of yesteryear. He had, in fact, spent several of his thirty-nine years living with Indians on reservations in Idaho and the state of Washington. It never occurred to me to ask while he was here, but maybe he is at least part Native American. I would say that Dan is not sociable, that he doesn't do well in formal settings or in large groups, but that he's very personable if he gets to know and like you. We got to know and, for the most part, like each other. Nevertheless, his obsessions—a fidgety need to work and an insatiable appetite for black coffee and sweets—conflicted with mine. This might have caused us to come to blows if he had spent the entire three months with me.

I was pleased that Dan quit smoking cigarettes when he came to Ford Arm. That eliminated one potential source of conflict between us. Unfortunately, he replaced one addiction with another. He would rise half an hour before me, make coffee, and drink the entire pot (three cups) before I could get any. I'd pour and all that spilled out were the grounds. By the end of the day, he'd have gulped down ten or fifteen cups to my two. So we were running short, and this irritated me a little.

Another irksome habit concerned toilet paper, that great equalizer of men and women, commoners and queens. Before we built our outhouse, we had to simply go plop in the forest as the bears do. (At least we buried ours.) Dan would grab the toilet paper from where we kept it dry on the enormous pile of equipment under sheets of plastic. Instead of taking only as much as he needed, he would carry the entire roll with him. Since it was usually raining or at least wet (dripping vegetation), the entire roll would come back one useless soggy wad.

One day I swallowed hard and broached my dissatisfaction over the coffee and the toilet paper with Dan. His response was a grunt. That was his last utterance to me for several days.

Then one morning I noticed him chop down a couple of dead hemlocks. All morning long he peeled the bark off the two logs with a little hatchet, a rather arduous process, bent over, chipping, chipping, chipping. "What's he doing?" I thought to myself. "Does he think we're building a log cabin here?" In fact our wall-tent was to be constructed with rough lumber already stock-piled in camp. I thought he knew that.

Finally, at lunch, my curiosity overcame my animosity. I asked him in as chummy a voice as I could muster, "What do you have in mind for those peeled logs, Dan?" He looked up from his sandwich and stared coolly at me while he chewed. Finally he said in a deliberate, calm voice: "I thought they'd look real nice shoved up your ass." "Sure, uh, where's the Vaseline?" I answered, trying to deflect his lingering hostility with a lame joke. But with that exchange at least we were on speaking terms again.

I can take only so much of a chain saw ripping apart the serenity of the wilderness. Dan just loved to run that thing, not for its own sake necessarily, because he was generally doing something productive, like cutting firewood. But I could never get over the impression that to him the buzz of the saw was part of the wilderness—music in the woods—whereas to me it represented a snarling mechanical intrusion, albeit sometimes a necessary one.

One morning I was trying to talk to Juneau on the radio while Dan was revving up the chain saw about twenty yards away. I could hardly hear my boss above the infernal noise. By coincidence, it was after this conversation that our radio ceased working. For more than a week Juneau was unable to make contact with us. Leon Shaul told me later that he could hear the saw whining in the back-ground, and that one of the last things he heard was me shouting: "Dan, would you turn off the chain saw while I'm on the radio!" When Shaul finally arrived with my new partner Detlef, he kidded that he had told the pilot to land on the lake only when they saw me come out alive to meet them on the raft, lest I had been the victim of an "Alaskan Chain Saw Massacre."

I don't think Dan ever finished high school, and this of course imparted an outlook on problem-solving (not to mention on life) that clashed to some extent with my own. I had three boxes of books to read; Dan didn't have a single one. His knowledge of science was haphazard, yet he still loved to hold forth on various aspects of geology or biology.

One of his most preposterous stories concerned what he claimed was a fossilized dinosaur egg that he once discovered in Washington. When he took it to the experts at the university in Seattle, he said, they scoffed at it and told him it was just a round rock. Discouraged but not defeated, he took it home. There he attempted in vain to bring it to life by fertilizing it himself. I nodded and tried to maintain my serious expression. "Maybe it was rotten after all these years," I suggested solemnly. As you can see, I often either had to bite my tongue or risk injuring the pride of a man twelve years my senior.

During the construction of our wall-tent, our work roles underwent somewhat of a reversal. I had expected him to take the lead because he had so many more practical skills and experience than I. And he did take the lead initially. Early on, though, it became apparent to both of us that he had a poor concept of our product and how to design it, so I found myself in command.

It was sad really, for I could see and feel his spirit sag. Without a word ever being spoken, we both realized that I'd taken over a domain of his. I know how tough it is on your sense of dignity and self-worth when someone moves in on your area of expertise, or proves you wrong again and again. It's even tougher when that someone is younger than you and already has it over you in other areas. Dan seemed a bit defeated and grew more taciturn for a few days.

Dan could be as stubborn as a stone, persisting at some task long after you knew that it would have to be undone. Whereas I tended to inaction or paralysis borne of uncertainty, Dan was a doer, a man of action. He really missed his century. Building railroad tracks across the virgin continent was his true calling. He tackled work with a gusto even if he was doing it wrong. Of course, this sometimes led to tension between us.

Other memories of Dan are more pleasant. He was a great one for campfires. Before we installed our oil-burning stove, fires were the only means of drying out wet clothes and warming up quickly. Even as early as late August, some days were raw and miserable, especially standing up to your waist in the stream wrestling salmon. Dan diligently tended the fire on such days, and believe me, it was a godsend for benumbed fingers.

Almost every evening, we toasted ourselves beside the crackling fire as the somber woods filled with darkness. It was during these "fireside chats" that I warmed up to Dan and learned of his personality and his past. He told me of his wild youth, of his earlier bout with alcoholism, of his experiences in Vietnam and Southeast Asia, of being thrown into jail in the Aleutian Islands because he had grabbed another man, put him in a headlock, and cut off his long hair. Against the man's wishes, of course.

In his wistful, rambling way he spoke also of his two failed marriages, and of the eight-year-old daughter he had by his second wife who lived in Washington and whom he hadn't seen in a couple of years. Apparently his ex wouldn't let him anywhere near her. He chuckled about this, but the sadness showed through. Sometimes Dan would expound on some subject that he claimed to have studied, and then admit he didn't really know what he was talking about after a fifteen-minute discourse.

Dan frequently talked or hummed to himself, sometimes old Indian chants or tunes he'd learned during his days on the reservations. Halfway through one black night he raised me with a shout. (We slept in separate nylon back-packing tents before the wall-tent was erected.) He'd heard splashing in the stream and was sure it had to be a bear.

Awakened and alarmed now, I heard it too—single plops, not prolonged splashing or swishing through water. I was not convinced it wasn't just spawning sockeye salmon, but "woodsy" Dan seemed pretty certain, and this frightened me. He fired his .44 Magnum. Two bursts rent the still black air. For one hopeful minute the splashing ceased. But only for a minute. Then it resumed, low-key but persistent, unintimidated by our display of firepower.

Later, as I drifted into a restless sleep, hand on my loaded shotgun, Dan chanted an old Indian bear song, contrived who knows how long ago, to ward off bears. He wasn't chanting it merely to celebrate or remember an earlier culture; it was clear to me that he really believed in its power. Despite my anxiety, I couldn't help but feel enchanted by the timelessness of the situation.

Tlingit Indians, a Native American tribe still found in southeast Alaska, had lived and died in this region. Perhaps their spirits would watch over and protect us.

After Dan left for Juneau, I felt a sort of pity or empathy for him—that he was entering middle age and still had no niche in society, that he was such a loner (though who's to say if he's actually lonely?), and that he was so oblivious to the reputation his appearance and social awkwardness created.

My new partner is a young, twenty-three-year-old long-haired German immigrant to the United States named Detlef Büttner. (Judging by what Dan did to the other long-hair in the Aleutians, it's probably fortunate for Detlef that I'll be his partner and not Dan!) I'll tell you more about Detlef later.

A plane is supposed to arrive later today to replenish our dwindled food supplies, though I doubt if it'll make it through; the sea mists are moving in again, totally sealing us off from the rest of the world. In any case, I'll continue writing and send this to you at first opportunity. I'll add it to the stack of thirteen other letters I'm sending out on this plane run. There are still many friends who haven't the slightest idea that I'm no longer in Juneau.

Life has become much more relaxed and routine here since my last writing. There are fewer building projects, and at the moment, fewer fish through the weir as a result of an improvement in the weather. I've actually had time to indulge in my favorite pastime—sitting in our newly constructed outhouse, gazing at the woods and reading! My partner has already remarked that he does not expect to see me for at least fifteen minutes when I disappear with a book and a wad of toilet paper. I told him that he's now getting to know the real me.

The better weather has also meant that the extensive alpine areas (above timberline) around us are accessible. In the past two weeks we've gone on four hikes in the high country. Our camp sees only a narrow slot of open sky, nestled as it is in a gap in the hills through which a stream drains Ford Arm Lake. The sky is blotted out too by the tall stands of hoary spruces and hemlocks. Walking through valleys means thrashing through dense growths of devil's club and its spiny stem, twigs, and leaves, as well as other brush. Thus, it's a total delight bordering on ecstasy to be able to glide freely over the carpet of tiny alpine plants, to see the open sky again, and to have some elbow room.

Also, the views of the country we're surrounded by are superb. We have a topo map that permits us to pick out topographic features. It's really fun to learn the lay of the land, to know that in this valley we discovered a tall waterfall and that on that mountainside we saw ten deer.

I'm much less apprehensive about the countryside now than I was when I arrived. At first it seemed oppressive—we were surrounded (as much in my imagination as in reality) by impenetrable forests, ceaseless rain and clouds, stark cliffs, and scowling bears. My sense of freedom was very circumscribed. Now, after five weeks here and a certain amount of exploring, I've surpassed those earlier psychological limits. My perception of our surroundings has changed.

I am developing a feeling for the different forces at work here, for what is possible and what isn't, a sense of proportion. I'm learning what it means to operate a fish weir and survive in the Alaskan wilds.

Above timberline we also attain excellent views to the west. There the mountain ridges tumble down to the ocean and an intricate fringe of islands—the Myriads they're called—provides the perfect transition between the continent and this remote reach of the sea. When we gaze westward we see the southern Gulf of Alaska, on the other side of which, over five hundred miles distant, are Kodiak Island—home to the largest brown bears on earth—and the Aleutian Islands. There are three very splendid, lofty mountains on the Khaz Peninsula that grace our view, between which you can see the shimmering afternoon waters beyond. We've nicknamed these peaks and the passes between them the "Gateway to the Gulf."

As I alluded to earlier, we see deer by the dozens in these areas. There's lots of good grazing to be done there, I guess, before the bad weather and snows close off the high country for the season. Then they descend into the forest. These deer don't seem to know what to do when they detect us. Could it be, really, because they've never seen people before? We nearly stepped on one eight-point buck, who stood within ten yards of us, in full view, looking uneasy, but not doing much about it.

Back at camp I must admit we're having some uninvited shaggy visitors. There are at least two bears that have been frequenting our site, scrounging for fish in the stream and in our garbage, before I started hoisting it up a tree. We saw bears in camp here originally, but then they disappeared for weeks and I reckoned they were giving us a wide berth. But I guess the lure of good food is too much for any self-respecting *Ursus*.

Several mornings now I've opened the door to our wall-tent to be greeted by a bear not twenty yards away. One morning I watched while one ambled leisurely up the gravel pathway from the river, lay down, yawned, scratched his (her?) nose, and took its sweet old time walking upstream again when it noticed my partner and me watching it—the perfect picture of nonchalance. No reason to rush through life when you're a grizzly, and nothing (save man) challenges you, and there's food within reach everywhere you look or sniff.

Another time, one moseyed into our "front yard" and up to a little pit where we'd burned some garbage the day before. First he sniffed whatever remained of the odors; then he lay down on his back right in the pit and began rolling around like a dog playing in the snow, rubbing all those choice smells into his coat. For clinchers, he ambled leisurely over to a tree, where he stood up on two legs, back pressed against the trunk, and scratched his back by moving up and down. He looked over toward me with the mellow expression of someone in the middle of a very pleasurable back rub. Tough life.

At first, having bears so close was very disturbing, especially at night, when each splash or crunch would elicit from one of us, "Did you hear that? What do you think it was?" The answer was implicit in the question. But it was almost as if we believed that by not naming what we knew it had to be, somehow the monster itself wouldn't actually materialize.

We'd lie there feeling uncomfortable and very vulnerable and very alone, stricken by man's primordial fear of bear. And a very ancient fear that must be. Who knows how many thousands of generations of scrawny *Homo sapiens* have trembled at the sight or sound of the mighty bruins? And the only weapons our ancestors had were fire, stones, and spears, plus their wits and courage. For us here, even with modern firearms, stepping out into the darkness to take a pee was an act of supreme courage at first. I kept a loaded shotgun beside my sleeping bag.

Well, we're adjusted to the point where the other day I went to work fixing something on the weir with a grizzly just 30 yards away in the bush feeding on a fish. It's part of developing a sense of the proportion of things that I mentioned, in this case getting a feel for the degree of danger represented by these particular bears, what a safe distance is, recognizing whether they are calm or agitated, and so forth.

Many times in my mind I've compared this familiarization process with that which occurs when we learn to drive a car. Each day, a car driver comes within split seconds and precious few inches of death, yet this fact no longer unnerves us or chokes our ability to take action. And despite fifty thousand auto deaths each year, most of us do avoid serious injury.

What you have to watch for is growing careless to the risks, and the same is probably true here. Overall, seeing bears is part of what a wilderness experience is all about. Without the bears, this country would be so much pretty scenery, nothing more than a lovely but empty landscape. I feel incredibly privileged when I consider how few people will ever, can ever, in this modern age, see wild brown bears in this uncorrupted setting pursuing their inimitable ursine existence. It's quite different from sitting in a car on a road in Yellowstone National Park watching the bears panhandle junk food from other tourists.

Four species of salmon spawn in this stream, the lake, and the smaller streams that feed the lake: the chum or dog salmon, the pink or humpback, the sockeye or red, and the coho or silver. Most of our work centers on the coho, although we have to record where and when we see the other species as well. Nature is unkind to the salmon, at least from our perspective. Whereas other fish are anadromous, or return to breed in fresh water, the salmon's reward for fulfilling its biological obligation is death. Most other fish, I believe, can spawn more than once. Not the Pacific salmon. For the ten percent or so that survive and return from their journey to the sea to spawn here, this is the short, short climax of their lives, and they die soon after spawning, within several days or a week.

By that time they have become covered with brown fungus. Chunks of skin have sloughed off, revealing their raw flesh underneath. Bones protrude. Frequently, before they die but after they are too weak to resist anymore, the gulls pick out their eyes. I have found pink salmon with both eyes missing still striving blindly against the current, still barely able to hold their place. Perhaps at that stage they don't even feel pain anymore. Certainly they don't possess the horror we feel at the thought of our own eyes being plucked out while we are still alive.

Those cohos that are fresh from the sea can be a magnificent sight: males and females in their primes, up to almost a yard long and weighing in at ten to twenty pounds, their scales glistening. Both sexes turn reddish beneath and develop a snout. The males are redder and have a snout that is more pronounced and toothier. In a shallow pool below the weir, at least three hundred cohos are waiting for higher water to move upstream. They are packed so tightly you can't see the stream bottom. Patiently waiting. Or at least it appears patient. Maybe they are impatient for all I know. Maybe neither. We can look down on them from a bank and occasionally you see one suddenly dart through the mass, snapping its jaws and sometimes leaping clear of the water. Perhaps these are the impatient ones.

It's disappointing though, in a way, to examine the fish more closely in hand and see how many are wounded or scarred. Most commonly a flap of skin on the jaw is hanging loose, but often enough we see more gruesome sights: a hook protruding from a blinded eye, a gaping wound on the belly. Always I wonder: what does it mean to the fish? Do they know pain as we do?

I have to jab the fish under the dorsal (back) fin with a needle and insert a tag there. When we were just starting out, apparently we weren't using enough anesthetic, for the fish would often wriggle and squirm violently when I inserted the needle. I would grimace myself. Now that they're more heavily dosed, they show no sign of pain.

Our handling has seemingly caused other problems too—about a dozen fish have drifted back to the weir roughly a week after we tagged them. Large blotches of some sort of fungus or mold cover those parts of the body where we appear to have inadvertently wiped off scales or the fish's protective slime. These sorry-looking specimens linger for a few days in our vicinity, as if to haunt us, and finally die. It makes you feel pretty disgusted with yourself to know you are at least in part responsible. And yet I certainly do not believe that what we are doing here is wrong—collecting data on a living renewable resource so it can be more intelligently exploited by humanity without being destroyed.

I guess I am just bothered at times by my own willingness, and that of other people, and even more so Nature's, to treat an individual life as expendable. Once I saw a brownie swat a humpy (pink salmon) onto a gravel bar and take a large chomp right out of the hump on the pink's back. At that moment a larger chum salmon splashing through the shallows caught the bear's eye. Abandoning the pink, it lunged for and grabbed the fat, juicy chum. The hapless pink, meanwhile, lay forgotten on the gravel, flopping in agony. But Nature's own cruelty is a philosophical conundrum that I won't probe any further now.

One other animal that occupies a prominent place in our daily lives here is the raven. It's probably my favorite bird. If they aren't really intelligent, they sure put on a good show of it. We hear and see them every day frequently flying up the cleft the stream cuts through the trees, uttering their hoarse croaks and gurgles. They display a repertoire of odd sounds and every now and then come up with a new one I haven't heard before. As they fly by you can hear each swish of their wings. On our hikes, we often see these aerial acrobats cavorting in the air like kids playing tag. It's marvelous to watch the movement of their wings and connect it to their flight patterns. When they tuck their wings under, they dive precipitously. At times I am certain they are following us, perhaps like a dolphin following a ship.

Ny new partner, Detlef, does a lot on his own initiative without consulting me, but willingly and enthusiastically conforms to my will on more important matters. He has an excellent command of English and we have long, fascinating discussions on almost everything. It's interesting to hear his interpretations of presentday Germany and European youth. He loves to hike as much as I do and has a much stronger affection for fish than I.

We've been together alone for over three weeks now. Detlef is a volunteer and the only remuneration he's receiving is college credit for his time and effort here. There's no problem at all with him feeling dissatisfied at my being paid and his not for doing essentially the same things. He's new to this area of North America—a pilgrim as it were—and is very grateful to be having such an experience and not having to pay for it. In Europe, of course, country this wild disappeared centuries ago, and so he appreciates how extremely fortunate it is for a European to experience genuine wilderness and not pay a stiff price for the privilege.

Detlef knows how to play the harmonica, and in the evenings around the campfire or inside by the glow of lanterns, I enjoy this simple sound that has so long been associated with the outdoors, and especially the West. Last night for the first time I brought out my recorder and played some melodies as I waited for some washed clothes to dry above a fire. I discovered that we have excellent acoustics here, from the steep hill just across the stream. Each note has a slight echo. You'd think we were in a recording studio or Carnegie Hall. Now all I have to do is learn to play!

Our wall-tent is almost as snug and luxurious as a cabin, and I find myself calling it that. It is spacious and well-lit, not cramped and dark like the backpacking tents I'm so familiar with. A three-burner camp stove rests at one end of the table. Every evening we pump it up and every couple of days we pour in more stove fuel, using a small funnel. Shelves line the walls and hand tools hang down from their nails. For decor, maps of Alaska and British Columbia and USGS quadrangles of Chichagof Island are attached to the studs above my study area. A number of the books I brought are lined up in one corner, almost enough to constitute a "library"; well, a traveling library anyway. It's all very homey.

We make our own hours, doing our chores whenever we want, by our own clocks. I can't claim we operate according to Nature's clock, for we don't rise with the dawn and retire with dusk. If anything, I've retreated to my old college habits of rising late and working late. Only when the fish come is our schedule dictated by an outside force. Otherwise, we follow our whims, just as I can imagine Indians of old on this coast did during plentiful seasons. It's not that we're undisciplined; hell, I've put up a chinning bar to demonstrate that! We're simply not rigid. That's one of the fringe benefits of an offbeat job like this that attracts bohemians like me.

As our foodstuffs have rotted, gone sour, or been eaten one by one, our diet has become simplified. Coffee, Kool-Aid, and pancakes have replaced peanut butter, fruit juice, and oatmeal as staples. Yesterday the last egg went, so today we had pancakes without eggs, which the recipe calls for. Tomorrow the last of the powdered milk will disappear, then our pancakes will consist of flour and water. We're wondering what they will taste like when the flour runs out. With luck, a plane will arrive first, but if not, there's always fish, although fish and water on the frying pan will probably produce lousy pancakes. Ah, the joys of the simple wilderness life!

You've heard the expression, "If life gives you lemons, make lemonade"? Well, we've been given the Alaskan equivalent — salmon — and so have come up with the local equivalent to lemonade — smoked salmon. We rigged up an improvised smoker out of spare materials, and for wood we use peeled alder sticks instead of the preferred hickory. It works, but it's a nuisance because you want to *smoke*, not *bake* the salmon steaks. The sticks are always either bursting into open flame or going out, neither of which is satisfactory. We've had to tend it an entire day, and even so, our product is not exactly choice smoked salmon. It was cooked too much and it gives me heartburn. But edible it is, so we won't starve, just get bored to death.

Well, this sheet is running out of lines, so I'll call it quits. You can expect another transmission of my crazed thoughts in several weeks' time, if and when the next plane ever deigns to pay us a visit. I trust all's well with you — if not the world.

Love,
Leon

*

September 21   *9 A.M. water level 66 centimeters*
                                 9 A.M. water temp. 52.5 degrees F

Weather: mild and partly sunny

The continuing food shortage has forced us to be original and experiment with different foods and combinations thereof. We discovered that tortillas and leftover salmon seasoned with mayonnaise, tartar sauce, and soy sauce is a good combo.

No major events today; only 4 chums in trap.

Detlef did some fishing at the mouth of inlet stream B today and says he noticed a number of very dark cohos leaping near the mouth.

September 22   *9 A.M. water level 64.5 centimeters*
                                 9 A.M. water temp. 52 degrees F

Weather: overcast & dismal-looking; slight drizzle in afternoon & breeze. Not enough to raise water level.

Food outlook is getting grimmer by the day. Before too long I fear we'll take forks and knives to each other. Only our good humor, iron wills, and infinite patience sustain us. The sounds of small planes overhead tormented us today. We ran outside and listened to each, fingers crossed, daring to hope against all odds that one would grow louder and appear over the ridge, rescuing us from our abject misery, but each sound faded away. In keeping with its past record, the radio would not communicate today for reasons unknown, despite a battery more charged than the ionosphere. Our plight was our own.

The fish continued to hold out for higher water. None at all in trap today.

There was a modest aurora (northern lights) last night. Detlef had never seen one before and stood out in his underwear in the cold for 5 minutes gazing at the shifting green curtains of light overhead. As we stood there beside the weir, a small weasel-like critter scurried past on an errand of its own, probably a mink.

At dusk today I saw a bear on the east shore of the lake about 250 yards from camp unobtrusively going about its own business. Although I should know better by now, I am still continuously surprised at how little commotion they generally stir up in their travels. Somehow you think of bears causing a big stir wherever they go, but more typically they fit right into their surroundings. This, of course, can make detection of them difficult. And avoidance!

September 23   *9 A.M. water level 79 centimeters*
                                  9 P.M. water level 97 centimeters

Weather: light rain and overcast skies all day

The waters rose slightly today in response to rains that started early in A.M. Fish responded too; we are back in business. Just as we finished with fish in early eve, lo! our delivery plane was almost upon us. We hurriedly got things together to go out and meet the pilot. Nonburnable garbage, letters, and data were all snatched up for the flight out.

Later, opening the boxes was like being a kid on Christmas morning again. The most thrilling discovery of all was a bag of mousetraps! Only problem was that once we had inventoried everything and compared it to our list, there were several major omissions. That's the problem with trying to order food over the radio when reception is marginal. "Ten" can easily sound like "two" at the other end!

September 24   *11 A.M. water level 84.5 centimeters*
                                  11 A.M. water temp. 51 degrees F

Weather: mild and breezy with high overcast all day; no rain; water dropping after yesterday's rain

A number of cohos milling below the weir today but few willing to enter the trap.

Saw a brown bear in evening at opposite end of weir, crunching fish. Probably the same brownie we've been seeing. No problems still.

There were over 30 dead sockeyes against the weir this morning, and much other debris of the season—fallen leaves and needles carried by the wind.

Last night we tried out our new mousetraps, baited with (what else but) cheese. I set one up right by the door, thinking I'd intercept a mousie even before it reached the table. I was right. Scarcely had I blown the lantern out when I heard a snap down on the floor, followed immediately by 20 seconds of frenzied rattling. By the time I'd leapt down with my flashlight, the little tyke had stopped twitching.

Above: Ford Arm Lake from our campsite.
Below: Ford Arm and the Myriad Islands.

Above: The wall-tent from our campsite.
Below: A brown bear devouring salmon.

Above: Our connection to the outside world: floatplane on Ford Arm Lake.
Below: A brown bear using sandbags as a footpath.

Above: Detlef hiking above timberline.
Below: A brownie in the weir trap.

Above: A hiking scene in the high country above Ford Arm.
Below: A brownie peering out of the foliage toward the weir;
note the characteristic head shape.

Above: A male coho in spawning condition.
Below: Two cohos. The silvery one is fresh from the ocean; the deep red one has been in fresh water longer and is ripe to spawn.

Above: Dead salmon washing up against the weir.
Below: The weir in flood. Note the salmon in foreground.

Above: Painting of a coho by Detlef Büttner.
Below: A chum salmon spawned out and dying in the shallows.

I tossed the dead mouse outside and reset the trap, placing it down on the floor gently so as not to trip it. Before I had so much as stood up, I saw another unsuspecting country-bumpkin mouse, dainty *Peromyscus,* slip through the door. I held my breath and froze. It pattered forward to the very edge of the mouse trap, whiskers protruding and snout sniffing.

Innocent little relative of the detested house mouse, this deer mouse was at home on the forest floor among the moss and fallen conifer needles. It was out of its element on our plywood floor, up against the superior technology of contemporary mousetraps. I began to feel sympathy for the little creature, but still I gazed in morbid curiosity, not tipping it off to the cruel fate that lay a whisker away.

Then it extended its snout right up to the cheese and began nibbling, directly under the swoop of the spring-loaded wire. It was like a person gorging on steak under a guillotine. For a couple of seconds it chewed contentedly, then it made the fatal mistake—it tugged at the cheese. The wire bar flipped around and caught the *Peromyscus* on the neck. It let out a pathetic squeak and jerked about like a hyperactive toy for ten seconds. It wasn't a pretty sight really, unless you're the sort who liked to torture flies as a child. I didn't reset the trap.

September 25

9 A.M. water level 74.5 centimeters
9 A.M. water temp. 51 degrees F

Weather: high overcast A.M.; partly sunny P.M. This was the warmest day we've had in a while. Swarms of no-see-ums were bothersome in the midday.

Walked the inlet streams today, each one to the likely limit of salmon movement. No activity in any.

Last night at 1 A.M. we heard a terrible scraping sound in the direction of the weir. I walked out to investigate, lantern and flashlight in one hand, shotgun in the other. Two pale orange eyes examined me from the catwalk, halfway across the weir. They blinked out, and I saw the form of a bear plod away from me as I walked up the catwalk. The bear (large and dark) continued downstream, huffing and grumbling a little as it went.

The sound was that of our tub of water in the trap being pushed across our platform. To my knowledge, this is the first time a bear has been in our trap itself. This morning the tub was upset again when I emerged from the tent. Hope this action doesn't signal a breakdown of the détente that now exists between bear and man at Ford Arm.

This morning our regular brownie was in the water just upstream of the weir. When it sensed me, from about 40 yards off, it popped its jaws several times before moving slowly away.

September 26

> 10 A.M. water level 69 centimeters
> 10 A.M. water temp. 51 degrees F

Weather: no precip.; continuing mildness & high overcast with some sun in afternoon

Walked to tidewater today, exactly one week after last trip there. Spawning activity by pinks and chums below the weir has plummeted. We saw fewer than one dozen chums, and pinks may have numbered only a couple of hundred or so.

Bear on the catwalk again last night, about 11 P.M. Again I drove it off. Not sure if it's the same, or if this bear is one of the two visitors we have distinguished.

Halfway through the night I was awakened by a series of eerie, half-human calls that drifted in from somewhere in the darkened forest. Had never heard anything quite like it before and can't say even whether it was bird or beast.

September 27

> 9 A.M. water level 67.5 centimeters
> 9 A.M. water temp. 50.5 degrees F

Weather: indecisive—several outbursts of rain & a good deal of sun; windy on ridges, gusty down on lake. Air temp. lower. A very fall-like day.

We placed one of our mousetraps on the first step below the door last night and this morning it was gone. Some animal is wandering around wearing a mousetrap.

I seem destined to be jinxed with incessant radio troubles. This morning reception was poor (what else is new?) and I could not reach the commercial fisheries office in Juneau, although I did speak with a technician at the radio repair shop just outside of town. Right afterwards, as I was disconnecting the battery from the radio to charge it yet again (I had just done so late last week), I was startled by sparks between the red and green wires and the positive terminal, from which I was removing them. The radio was still hooked up but the set was turned off. The ground wire was still attached to the negative terminal post.

Later, the set didn't start at all when I reconnected everything. I spent 2½ hours tinkering with it before giving up in disgust. Saw something that might be the trouble, but I didn't want to mess with it lest I worsen things.

This afternoon in a walk around the lake, Detlef saw what sounds like a family of otters. Later, in the woods a short distance from camp along lake, I saw what were probably two minks.

September 28

9 A.M. water level 67.5 centimeters
9 A.M. water temp. 49 degrees F

Weather: dawned clear & bright with small pockets of mist; 9 A.M. air temp. was 35 degrees F. Later warmed considerably, into sixties.

Radio still out of order.

The brown bear is still hanging around, finishing off sockeye carcasses. Saw him this morning; he moved away as I went to the weir.

I believe I hear a bear outside right now. Some bear left a large turd last night in the middle of our gravel path just a few feet up from the steps at the water's edge. It was the color of the gravel (blue-gray), which explains why Detlef stepped in it.

No sockeyes (alive) anymore in front of camp. Spawning finally appears over. Fewer dead ones appearing at weir, too.

*

Chichagof Island
September 28, 1982

Dear Ma and Pa,

Although a plane delivery isn't due for a couple of more weeks, I thought I would start a letter to you now and add bits 'n pieces as time and events permit.

Ever since I sent off my last letter to you, five days ago, I've been bothered that what I said about bears may make you worry unnecessarily. Perhaps I omitted several things that would assuage any fears you may have. First, I should have emphasized, if I did not, the passivity and subordination of all the bears we've encountered so far. If there's ample distance between us, they simply go about their business, completely unperturbed; if not, they always back off. In fact, I've been amazed at how quiet and inconspicuous they are. You naturally expect bears to cause a commotion wherever they go. Not so.

Second, this is by no means the first time I've ever been in bear country. Virtually all of my outdoor activities in the west have put me in grizzly bear range—the four-week kayak trip up the British Columbia coast, two-week canoe trip down the Yukon, and countless shorter outings. Not once have I had trouble with bears, although I've seen quite a few.

Third, I think other risks inherent in the pursuit of outdoor activities are greater than wild-animal encounters. My kayak voyage, with its possibility of capsizing in a frigid ocean, was far more dangerous than my present situation, which is like sitting at home watching TV by comparison. I think there is a higher probability of choking on a fish bone than being attacked by a bear.

There, I hope you rest easier now (if you were ever anxious at all). I feel quite calm about the whole thing and in fact enjoy knowing the bears are around. They are what help make this country living wilderness and not merely sterile scenery.

September 29, 1982
Wednesday

Yesterday was a beautiful Indian summer day, such as they occur at all on this coast. Autumn is definitely not the season to first experience southeast Alaska. While other regions have bright, crisp days and brilliant colors that can make it exhilarating to be out of doors, all we get here to mark the passage of the seasons is dreary rainfall and dwindling daylight.

So, we took advantage of the conditions and went on a long hike. Climbed a small (seventeen hundred feet) mountain and reached a particular unnamed lake for the first time. The lake is about three miles in circumference and is at elevation 423 feet. It appeared pretty lifeless, unlike the lake we are on, and is more open, not nearly as shut in by the hills and forest as ours. Given the remote setting, it was strange to see a Chevron oil barrel, not even very rusty, resting on the lakeshore.

We have to bushwhack on these hikes, as there are no trails except for those made by the animals over the centuries, which often come to abrupt ends. It's amazing how often they go the way you want to for a little while, though, and how well you can link them together.

Bushwhacking in the lowlands here almost requires a machete, which we sometimes carry. Alder thickets line many stream banks and much of the lakeshore. They can be quite dense. A fruit-bearing shrub called salmonberry also grows near streams.

The accursed devil's club is notorious among hikers in the Pacific Northwest for being strategically located right where you need to grab something urgently. Invariably, it seems, whenever you skid as you're crossing a slippery log and reach out impulsively to grasp the nearest branch and avoid a bruising fall, you grab devil's club . . . and a fistful of spines. Other times it seems to stage an ambush. You look around and the forest is open and inviting; before you know it, you're trapped in an impenetrable spiny thicket.

Devil's club spines can become embedded in your skin and get infected if not extracted. Not only are the woody stalks or stems lined with spines, but also the leaf stems and the undersides of the leaves themselves. I've entertained myself more than one night digging the tiny spines out of my palm and fingers with my knife. Your hand is left with dozens of little pit marks.

At a higher elevation than devil's club but still below timberline, the main understory bush is the blueberry, which is not so intimidating, and, of course, offers a certain reward.

Today is more typical of fall here, I suppose. The wind is blowing curtains of fine rain down the lake. Visibility is limited, for the clouds have engulfed us. The forest is green and dripping. We are closed in, shut off from the rest of the world. Our radio is broken down yet again, so we really are totally severed from the rest of humanity.

The tendency of things to break down or require constant maintenance is one of the most trying features of this job. This is the third time now we've had radio troubles. Not only does it cause unnecessary anxiety, but it means we're unable to order supplies we may need.

Well, at the moment the sky has lifted slightly and I can distinguish the mountain at the end of the lake, the one we ascended yesterday. The veil of mist and rain has thinned. However, our camp is still concealed from the gaze of the world. Time moves so slowly here. Only the fact that I've kept count and know the calendar date assures me I've been here almost two months now.

Except for the weather, each day is the same. There are no weekends to punctuate the passage of time; no TV or radio or newspapers to inform you of daily events, no meetings with other people to keep you abreast of their affairs. Overall, only the slow processions of natural cycles and events mark the movement of time: the spawning and dying of the sockeyes; the arrival of the cohos; the colder temperatures and the shorter days. I imagine it's a lot like what the early explorers and settlers of this continent knew, scattered as they were across the wilderness, out of touch with other people before modern communications linked everyone far and wide. Even events as significant as, say, the death of a parent or sibling, you might hear of only weeks or months afterward.

> *Love,*
> *Leon*

*

September 29
　　　　　　　　　9 A.M. water level 65.5 centimeters
　　　　　　　　　9 A.M. water temp. 49 degrees F
　　　　　　　　　11 A.M. water level 105 centimeters

Weather: rain all day, sometimes heavy; visibility poor (foggy)

I have been writing a good deal to my parents. Just finished trying to calm any worries that may have arisen over an earlier letter recounting bear episodes. I wish I actually felt as sanguine about bears as I have tried to make them feel!

I scarcely stuck my head outside the tent today but to check on the weir and visit the outhouse. It began raining fitfully in the morning and more steadily as the day wore on. The water level has risen, but as of this writing (11:30 P.M.) not enough to entice more than a few fish into the trap. It seems like it is taking higher water now to get the cohos to move upstream at all. Many of the cohos we tagged earlier came into the trap when the water level was below 100 centimeters. Yet now, with hundreds just downstream, they do not.

September 30

1:30 A.M. water level 130 centimeters

6 A.M. water level 180 centimeters

10 A.M. water level 169 centimeters

3 P.M. water level 145 centimeters

5 P.M. water temp. 49 degrees F

Weather: storming and horrendous gusting at night; heavy clouds & scattered bursts during day; cleared & lifted a bit later

Last night was the worst we have had here. Waters were rising from steady rain. By 1:30 A.M. was up to 130 centimeters but rain had slackened and I thought waters had nearly crested. We both retreated to our bunks for some sleep. But we got none, for the wind hurled itself at us with nightmarish ferocity; the whole frame shook and shuddered like a matchbox in a hurricane. The rain picked up too—but neither of us thought it was raining hard enough to produce the results it did.

At 4:45 A.M. I arose to have what I thought would be a routine look at the weir. I was astonished to discover that the flood waters had risen to within 1 inch of the tops of the pickets at the lowest part of the weir. I raced back, roused Detlef, and, maneuvering like acrobats, we secured the low sections of the weir by lantern-light. The rain had abated, but the wind had not. One gust blew my lantern over but I managed to grab it before it plunged into the flood.

As always, hundreds of Dolly Varden were backed right up to the upstream side of the weir. We were dismayed to see what appeared to be several cohos among them that may have gotten over the weir before we plugged it up. Alternatively, they could have leapt out of the trap, or drifted down from the lake, as the Dollys do in times of high water. Hard to say.

We have decided to simply leave the chicken wire in place from now on, as we can still negotiate the catwalk with it up.

In the morning the water was still too high and swift to work in the trap, which we had shut at 6 A.M. for fear of losing all the fish in it if the water rose much higher. We were faced with the dilemma of whether to open it and admit many fish while they were willing to enter and before they retreated back downstream as the waters fell. The risk of doing so was that if the waters rose again (and the weather was still uncertain) we could lose the whole trapful. We opted not to open the trap.

This proved to be the wrong decision, for the weather improved, the waters continued falling, and the fish became more reluctant to enter. We managed to sample 40 fish, but there are far more waiting to get upstream who seem to have backed off again.

It's now past midnight and I just checked the trap, in which we have some fish. If it's not one thing it's another—there were 2 bears in the bushes on the bank at the far end of the weir, just 15 yards from the trap. If they got in, they could wreak havoc on our fish. (Bears have *already* been in the trap at night, but when there were no fish.) May have to be vigilant again tonight.

*

September 30, 1982
Thursday

Dear Folks,

In at least two respects running this operation must be like running a farm or a ranch. You're depending on a variety of machines and tools—on your knowledge of how to use them, and on their not breaking down irreparably when you most need them. Secondly, you have to cope with that most capricious incarnation of Mother Nature—the weather.

It's a constant source of anxiety. Yesterday, we were hit with a deluge. It snuck up gradually, muting our senses. All day long the water level at the weir rose gradually. By evening the level was high, but not at flood stage. Then in the night the wind bore down on us in a fury, driving legions of rain against our battered tent.

When I got up and stepped out into the pitch blackness, with the trees swaying and the wind howling, I was startled at how the water had risen. We set to work immediately. It was quite a wild sensation, working so intently while the water rushed a foot below and the wind raged just above, our two lanterns blazing away keeping the darkness at bay.

After our hasty counterattack, I flopped onto my bunk for several hours rest. Now, at noon, the rains have abated and the wind isn't battering our tent any longer, but you can hear it above on the mountaintops, and the sky is still unsettled and ominous.

Love,
Leon

*

October

Dear Folks,

Years from now, I'll look back on this date and know that I spent it right where I am now. And I'll long desperately to be here again. I have to live in the present with the perspective of the future to get the most out of it.

It has always seemed to me, as I'm sure it has to every photographer, that I was never prepared for the best shots when fate presented them: either no film or no camera or inability to get the camera fast enough. Since I've been here I've missed two of the most incredible pictures ever.

The first missed opportunity occurred when my partner and I walked the mile downstream to Ford Arm itself. He fished for salmon at the stream mouth while I wrote you a letter as I sat atop a boulder. As we turned to start up the stream again, a wave of rain overtook us and, simultaneously, the air shimmered with a radiance that often precedes a rainbow. Sure enough, one did appear, and almost symbolically the arc dipped right into the entrance of the stream itself through a notch between the hills. Beyond the end of the rainbow was our rustic home.

Then, a bald eagle flew right through the colors of the spectrum, its white head brilliantly illuminated. I had taken the last shots on my roll of some damn mushrooms but moments before. My friend Detlef snapped one, but discovered later that he had his camera set for ASA 400-speed film, when in fact he had ASA 100 film inside.

Then, a couple of weeks ago, on one of our long hiking days, we paused for one last view from the heights of Ford Arm before the sun sank into the Pacific and we descended. The serene water was over two thousand feet below, and the ethereal play of clouds and light was so glorious that my heart ached, all the more, because once again I had just used up my film. Detlef proved himself once again—he had one picture remaining.

Just as he put the camera up to focus it, something almost magical happened. A deer—a buck with a proud rack of antlers—stepped cautiously into the foreground twenty yards away. He looked at us a moment, and then strutted in front of this sublime vista, and paused, or should I say *posed* there, while Detlef pressed his shutter button. Its duty fulfilled (furnishing us a "once-in-a-lifetime" photo opportunity), the deer continued on out of our sight. But I had fumbled fate's gift once again. Moments later, Detlef ripped his film as he rewound it, so that he may have blown it as well. Part of me smarts, and part of me says just that *being there* is what counts ultimately.

Love,
Leon

*

October 3

10 A.M. water level 107.5 centimeters
10 A.M. water temp. 48.5 degrees F
8 P.M. water level 99 centimeters

Weather: mixed clouds & sun with a few showers

Today we walked to tidewater. Pink and chum activity has now almost ceased entirely; we saw but a handful of each, although the deeper water and much swifter current hindered peering below the surface. It's surprising how quickly carcasses have disappeared. Guess most were washed out to sea in the recent flooding.

Cohos now seem more evenly spread out over 250-yard reach below weir. There are still hundreds, though it's impossible to gauge exactly how many. On our way downstream, we found a dead coho—still silvery. On our way up, we saw a single coho drift downstream looking healthy and maintaining equilibrium.

Saw a blackish (grizzly) bear at the edge of the meadow at tidewater. The brownish bear that hangs around the weir regularly was getting into the trap last night. He's beginning to be a nuisance.

On the most recent mail and food flight, a box of "birdshot" (shotgun pellets normally used to hunt small birds like doves and quail) arrived with the following message from our bosses:

> Use the birdshot if you have more trouble with bears only under the following conditions:
> 1. At least 40–50 yards (half a football-field length) between you and the bear.
> 2. Apply only to the bear's posterior; don't shoot if there is a chance of hitting the eyes.
> 3. The bear should run off never to return. However, it is still wise to be ready to take cover or defend yourself in the event that he reacts differently.

On point #3, I wish Leon and Phil had been a little more explicit on *how* we should protect ourselves!

October 4

11 A.M. water level 95 centimeters
11 A.M. water temp. 48 degrees F

Weather: overcast & occasional rain (drizzling & some outbursts)

One of our bears entered the trap again tonight and ran off with our only plastic bucket. Neither of us was willing to climb into the brush after the bear to retrieve it. Hope we can tomorrow in daylight. I'm on the verge of pumping birdshot into this bear's fat fanny, but it's not really feasible at night because we can't see it from 40–50 yards away well enough to aim accurately and not injure its eyes.

October 5   noon water level 89 centimeters
                                              noon water temp. 47 degrees F

Weather: last midnight the wind picked up & continued blowing nonstop until afternoon today. Gusts were not as powerful as on Sept. 30—for only the canvas & not the tent frame itself shook and shuddered—but still made sleeping rather uncomfortable.

Recovered the plastic bucket that was stolen last night by our furry friend. It was a little "chewed on" as Phil would say, but only two tooth punctures. Is still usable.

Midnight—the wind is howling and wailing again like a host of wraiths. Another wild and lonely night.

*

                                              October 5, 1982
                                              Tuesday

Dear Folks,

I have become an avid reader of *The Bulletin of the Atomic Scientists,* and in fact absconded with a number of discarded issues from my work library to keep me company here in the bush. *The Bulletin* is a monthly periodical founded in 1945, year of the birth of the "atomic age." It is a forum for ideas, opinions, and information on issues relating to human welfare and survival in the scientific age, and calls itself "the conscience of the international scientific community."

Its editors and contributors are the spiritual descendants of the likes of Albert Einstein and Leo Szilard, scientists and specialists concerned about the impact of science and technology on society. Here is an excerpt from an article entitled "Nuclear Ignorance," in the November 1981 issue:

> For atomic scientists and those working in related fields, the reality of nuclear weapons and the possibility of nuclear war is strong. But there is a new generation: forgetful, untutored. A high school student, 14 or 15 years old, whose

class I was visiting, approached me at the end of the hour. He was troubled by something that had been said during class:

"You say these things have been used before?"

"Yes. At Hiroshima and Nagasaki."

No response.

"In World War II."

A downward glance, his eyes serious, a little guarded:

"Huh, I had never heard that."*

*

October 6   *11 A.M. water level 91 centimeters*

11 A.M. water temp. 47 degrees F

Weather: light to heavy rainfall most of day; limited visibility

Noticed a number of cohos just below the weir today, but there were never more than one or two at a time disposed to enter the trap.

This evening, in full daylight, we saw a blackish bear waltzing along the 2nd row of channels on the weir as gracefully as a ballerina. It entered the trap once or twice. At one point, it lunged right from the trap platform into the water inside the trap; at a fish I reckon. It leapt out again immediately. We were both aware of how active and swift this bear was in comparison to the sluggish brownish bear that is a regular visitor. You could see the instant this bear detected our presence; sometimes I'm not sure by the brownish bear's behavior if it senses us or not. There may be more than 1 "brownish" bear for all I know.

Tonight, after dark, Detlef saw 2 pairs of bear eyes glowing on the bank at the far end of the weir.

---

*From THE BULLETIN OF THE ATOMIC SCIENTISTS. Copyright © 1981 by the Educational Foundation for Nuclear Science, 6042 South Kimbark, Chicago, Illinois 60637, USA. A one-year subscription is $30.

October 7

11 A.M. water level 101 centimeters
7 P.M. water level 95 centimeters
11 A.M. water temp. 47 degrees F

Weather: a moderate amount of rain mixed with a moderate amount of sun

Nothing new to report with fish.

Otherwise a very strange day—Christmas morning all over again. The sound of the plane swooping low overhead and landing was like out of a dream: we didn't expect another plane so soon. Dispatched 9 marked coho heads, mail, bum radio, and garbage; picked up mail, food, and fresh radio. The flights in here have become radio runs every bit as much as food runs. Much of the rest of the day was spent adjusting emotionally to the flood of personal news from outside.

Last night, after my journal entry, I saw what was probably the same blackish bear clowning around with our stack of sandbags. He looked like a feisty dog at play. I stood 12 yards away and watched with my flashlight; he didn't even seem to notice me. This morning saw our brownish bear on the weir and since dark this eve there's been the usual amount of activity out there.

October 8

noon water level 85.5 centimeters
noon water temp. 47 degrees F

Weather: no rain, but fog in A.M. & cloud ceiling about 2,000 feet P.M.

Walked each of the inlet streams today. There was no sign of coho in any stream. The water levels and current velocities in all 4 streams were down considerably from last week.

On our return journey in the raft we saw a bear along the shore of the southeast corner of the lake about 150 yards from camp.

October 9   7:30 A.M. water level 105 centimeters
                            10 A.M. water level 136 centimeters
                            2 P.M. water level 162 centimeters
                            8 P.M. water level 149 centimeters
                            2 P.M. water temp. 47 degrees F

Weather: started raining early A.M. (at night) & continued through night, morning & partly through afternoon. Blew like a gale in morn.

Quite a day. First—the rain we've been waiting for—just enough to fool the fish into believing they can get past, but not enough to top the weir. So we did a total of 161 cohos today. Most were dressed in breeding outfits.

Second—we had one mortality of a fish we'd just tagged due to a rather unusual, and I hope, one-time, cause. As the fish was recovering it fluttered along the weir towards the close shore 15 yards away and before it or we knew what had happened, one of our boorish bear friends scrambled down the bank and grabbed it. Actually, we knew the bear was up there and had been cautiously watching it watch us.

This action represents the greatest depredation to date, and I fear, signifies a growing boldness in the bears. Immediately after this, we began releasing the fish on the side of the trap away from the close bank. We also got the shotgun ready, first load with birdshot, 2nd buckshot, 3rd and 4th slugs—for warning, midrange, and point-blank range levels, respectively.

At one or two points, the bear started advancing to within 10–15 yards of us. It backed off—all of 5 yards—when I fired the gun into the air. Perhaps having to work with a loaded shotgun in the trap is a first for Coho Research. This bear seemed to be waiting till we left to move in.

Sometime in the afternoon I walked to the tent to retrieve something and ran across a blackish bear heading toward camp from the lake. It was about 30 yards away and withdrew when it saw me.

Later, after dark, Detlef was growled at by some unseen bear as he walked along our path about where the firepit is. He thought the sound came from somewhere down by the raft, about 15 yards away. It rattled him a bit. That's the first actual growl we've elicited. It's starting to feel like walking in a minefield or like we're members of an occupying army in hostile territory just waiting to be ambushed when we step outside at night. But still, there have been few occasions when it would've been possible to sting the bears with birdshot and still abide by the rules. Usually they're too close, or it's dark, or they're obscured in brush, or they're facing us. I have no desire to blind one because I was trigger-happy.

One thing we will stop doing is throwing some dead fish on the opposite bank. We'd been doing this (rather than tossing all into the water below weir) thinking that since they were attracted to the area generally, it was better to keep them on the opposite bank than on our side. But finding the fish we put there, as well as those that wash up there, may be one of the attractions in the first place. I wonder if any cohos have been caught by bears inside the trap?

Having an unreliable radio with so many bears around is not a situation to relish. If someone is hurt, we may not be able to call for help.

October 10   *11 A.M. water level 124 centimeters*
                                   11 A.M. water temp. 47 degrees F

Weather: heavy overcast & fog; rain on and off all day, at times heavy; water level still dropping slightly through day

Even with the water falling off, many fish still trying to move upstream. A good day for working, because of lower water and no winds.

More bear escapades today. Actually they began last night. At 4 A.M. our sleep was abruptly interrupted by deep growling. This isn't the first time we've heard growls, but except for what Detlef just heard the night before, it always came from the opposite side of the stream. This time it seemed much, much closer, like right outside our tent.

Still groggy with sleep, I sat up in my bunk wondering if I'd been dreaming. But in that instant I heard a bear's claw scrape the canvas of the wall-tent over by the table. I grabbed for the shotgun and shouted "Get the hell out of here!" Did the invader detect the quavering in my voice?

Who knows? But neither the growls nor the scraping resumed. What if we hadn't been here, if we'd been, say, off exploring somewhere? I'm almost positive, from their growing boldness, that we'd have returned to find our cabin a complete shambles.

Now the growing confidence around bears that I proudly wrote of to my parents is also in shambles. I slept poorly the rest of the night, troubled by nightmares about . . . what else? When we awoke in the morning I was determined that today we would draw a line in the mud and dare the bruins to cross it at their peril.

This resolve was strengthened when I stepped out the door and looked down to the stream. Something didn't look right. The raft was deflated! I ran down and saw that somebody (one guess who) had vandalized it. Claw marks and a gash more than a foot long left little doubt as to the culprit(s).

I heard scuffling on the far stream bank and looked up to see one of the bears nosing around. For the first time I didn't feel an excited "Wow! Isn't that neat!" reaction. My patience was shot. I trotted up to the cabin, grabbed the shotgun and slammed 4 shells into the chamber, 2 of birdshot followed by 2 of buckshot, just in case.

As I ran back down to the stream I told myself, "Remember to shove a shell in the chamber Leon! Remember to remove the safety, you idiot!"

The bear was still there, doing his own thing and more or less ignoring me. But where was he at 4 A.M. last night? I charged onto the weir and pounded swiftly across it. "Hey you! Git outta here! You're not welcome 'round here anymore!" I yelled. He turned his back to me, in contempt or complete disregard. Why should he heed me? My barks were toothless. But it was just the moment I'd been waiting for. Eyes safe. Maybe 35 yards between us. *Now!*

I planted the stock of the gun firmly against my shoulder, aimed, and pulled the trigger. It wouldn't budge. Damnation! I'd forgotten to remove the safety after all. I cursed and pressed the button and pulled the trigger again. Click, but no boom. Christ almighty, what a moron! In my nervousness at firing on a grizzly, I'd forgotten to shove a shell in the chamber too! If the bear had been charging me instead of minding his own business, that would've been my very last thought on Earth.

I quickly pumped a shell into the chamber, aimed at that furry rump as big as a barn side, and fired. *BOOM*. The reaction was instantaneous and unmistakable, unlike the languid response whenever we shouted, threw stones, or even fired the gun in the air. The bear jumped and shook as if a hundred killer bees had just buried their hot stingers into his fat butt. He tore along the bank downstream of the weir, and when he slowed down once, still facing away from me, *BOOM*, I fired again . Again he started, and this time he didn't stop at all. He ran along the stream, swam across it at record speed, and disappeared at a gallop around the bend.

Our other furry friend—of those we recognize—made his appearance in late afternoon, by the trap end of the weir. While we were getting ready up at the cabin to tag some fish, the bear advanced right to the trap. Still angry and determined, I decided the time was ripe to teach him a lesson too. No more Mr. Nice Guy. I rushed onto the weir with loaded gun and he began moving back toward the opposite end, grumbling.

While he was turned away, I let him have it, right in the rump, at a distance of about 40 yards, with one round of birdshot. He shook and ran off, but not quite never to return; rather, more like 10 yards before he stopped behind a tree. In a few minutes he was feeding again at water's edge, feeling for dead fish beneath the water with his paws, stretching his neck and lifting his chinny-chin-chin to keep his dainty head dry.

Well, we simply went to work in the trap while the bear fed peaceably 15 yards away. It made no attempt to approach us, but I can't say the birdshot made any obvious lasting impression. For our part, the gun was an arm's reach away, loaded once again with a mix of birdshot, buckshot, and slugs, in that order, corresponding to the increasing size and diminishing distance of a closing target. The gun makes it easier to concentrate on the fish instead of the 300-pound beast two hops away.

This morning a number (10?) of partially eaten Dolly Varden were washed against the weir. The work of an otter perhaps?

October 11

9 A.M. water level 102 centimeters
9:30 P.M. water level 145 centimeters
10:30 P.M. water level 160 centimeters
12 midnight water level 192 centimeters
9 A.M. water temp. 46.5 degrees F

Weather: gusts and moderate to heavy rain from noon on. By darkfall was almost a full-fledged gale.

There being no fish in the trap and with steady rainfall most of the day, I tried to catch up on my reading. Another slow day in the woods, the kind it's nice to be a grandpa in a rocking chair on. Where's my pipe and tobacco pouch?

Saw "The Bear" in the woods at the other end of the lake, but let him be. He gave us a wide berth, so maybe he's learned a lesson.

11 P.M.

The rain has intensified since darkness and the water just rose 15 centimeters in the last hour. We have the trap shut and all the chicken wire up to be safe at least to 10–20 centimeters higher than the high-water level to date (180 centimeters on Sept. 30), but the way this rain is driving, it will be a night for vigilance. Won't get fooled again . . .

In my most recent check, I saw a dense school of Dollys with some salmon among them just above the weir. I saw a blue tag on one salmon, meaning we'd passed it through and it has drifted down in the swifter current. This may or may not explain the several salmon we saw just above the weir on the Sept. 30 flood.

October 12

1 A.M. water level 210+ centimeters
3 A.M. water level 240+ centimeters
3 P.M. water level 183 centimeters
still falling through evening
5 P.M. water temp. 46.5 degrees F

Weather: rain all night with some gusts; drizzle most of day with periodic bursts of heavier rain

12:30 A.M.

Was out on the weir a few minutes ago placing sandbags on catwalk and tying down some more chicken wire. Found a dead tagged coho lying atop the catwalk—#9028 tagged on Aug. 24. It had several bites out of its belly. Otter? Bear? Was quite fresh. (I'd only been out an hour earlier and saw nothing.) The population of fish we tagged on the first day is being decimated by one thing or another!

1:20 A.M.

Just strung some more chicken wire over another portion of the weir. Water is now over the catwalk for 4–5 sections of the weir.

5 A.M.

Have been out for the last 2½ hours trying to brace weaker sections of chicken wire and remove debris. Debris collecting probably faster than we can discard it. Several sections of chicken wire were folded over under the weight of debris and force of current so that they were flush with the water surface. Can't tell if any cohos made it over; didn't actually see any the whole time out. By the trap the water is well over a foot above the catwalk; most of the catwalk under water. Water level seems to have crested, but now the rain, which never did stop, has intensified again.

8 A.M.

Am feeling burned out, like I've been through a battle. The weir itself—smattered with debris, still largely under water, fringed with floppy chicken wire—also looks like a fort under siege. Unfortunately, it's not clear that we held the fort in this battle, for we lost our grip in at least a couple of places.

I know now for a fact that fish got past the weir. First, in the morning at about 9:15, after a break in which I spoke to Leon on the radio, I saw a coho jump over the weir, in a place where the chicken wire was 1–2 feet above the water. In the next 15 minutes, while Detlef and I prepared to attach our last "reserve" roll of chicken wire there, I saw several others flop over.

Second, and more seriously, an unknown number of cohos squirmed through a bent part of the green vinyl-coated mesh on the bank at the camp end of the weir. At this point the wires had become separated as a result of a bear sitting on it or walking over it several days ago. When I first saw it then, I didn't repair it right away because it seemed inconsequential—it was above any foreseeable water level. So much for foresight as a dependable guide for action when it comes to floods. Now my complacency has cost us.

I stopped up the hole immediately with sandbags and later repaired it with extra mesh. The only estimate I can make on the number of escapees is "somewhere between 5 and 5,000." Should be nearer the lower figure, for only one fish could squirm and wriggle through at a time. Also, the hole was located in shallow, nearly still water, not in the mainstream, where most cohos seem to congregate in their quest to find passage upstream.

Detlef put the wet suit and mask on to check the sandbags along the bottom of the pickets, but the water was too turbid to see much.

Today I calculated that 85.3% of the adult cohos above the weir should be tagged, assuming no escapees and taking into account known mortalities.

We will compare the actual ratio of marked/unmarked in the spawning beds to this figure.

At the moment one or two bears are fishing right off the tilted upstream side of the weir. They apparently grub for the fish that get pushed up against the weir in floods. Not 5 minutes ago I heard a disconcerting row of grunting and growling, sounding perhaps like a cross between an angry elephant and a hungry lion. How lovely. Is it love or war? Hard to tell with bears.

These heart-stopping roars erupted periodically through the night. At one point I went out and checked. I saw 2 pairs of glowing orange eyes. One bear apparently charged the other while I walked on the catwalk, for it let out a deep, powerful bellow that froze me in my tracks. My blood turned thin. The gun felt good in my hands, but I can't help but wonder if I would even be able to use it effectively, were that terrifying growl directed at me from a charging bear 20 yards away. It makes a sixth-degree black-belt karate expert's preattack scream sound like a baby's whimper!

October 13

10 A.M. water level 122 centimeters

10 A.M. water temp. 46.5 degrees F

Weather: overcast & showers A.M.; beautiful partly sunny afternoon; some rain eve

Opened the trap A.M. and cleared it of any strays left inside from flood. (Seemed to be few or none.) Some fish still willing to enter trap despite falling water level. We noticed fish getting "ripe"—soft flesh and males squirt milt when pressed in belly. (Detlef seemed especially to enjoy this.)

Our Bear came 'round again this aft. Drove him back with stones. He was too close to shoot at from the trap and he wouldn't turn his back to us.

I haven't seen hide nor hair of the bear that galloped away when I peppered his bum with birdshot. Maybe he got the message.

October 14   *10 A.M. water level 93 centimeters*
                                        10 A.M. water temp. 46.5 degrees F

Weather: partly cloudy, partly sunny; no rain

Ford Arm Coho Research entered a new phase today with the first observation of spawning cohos. I first noticed several cohos just above the near end of the weir last evening waiting in shallow water. This morn they displayed characteristic breeding behavior, i.e., being paired up, turning on side and flipping of tail, and chasing away intruding fish.

I walked down to the pool 250 yards below the weir where the salmon have been massing and waiting for high water. The water was still too murky from the flood to see clearly; visibility was maybe 2 feet, but I could still see significant numbers of fish, certainly more than 100. I also observed perhaps a dozen cohos spawning *below* the weir, between it and the pool just referred to. I wonder how many more cohos we'll get through the trap now?

In the afternoon Detlef and I set out to walk the inlet streams, which I now felt certain would have spawning cohos. They did. With the raft wasted, we had to walk all the way along the lakeshore.

Stream A, the closest to camp, was the only one in which we conducted a fairly thorough search for cohos, and even in it, I'm sure we missed a number. Most of the cohos had to be driven from their hiding spots under banks and logs and stumps. It was quite laborious work; must've taken us 3–4 times as long to walk this stream as it took us before. It wasn't enough just to look carefully under banks; we had to swish sticks underneath and hope to scare them out.

We only walked about halfway up Stream B, for it was getting late. It is a much harder stream to survey, for it is larger and deeper, has many branches, and more logjams and banks difficult to probe with a stick. In the half-mile or so, we saw only 7 fish, far fewer than over a comparable distance in Stream A.

Streams C and D we only glanced at, since it was too dark to see properly.

We divided the cohos we saw into 3 groups: those that were definitely tagged, those definitely untagged, and those we were uncertain about. Here are the day's counts by stream:

	Tagged	*Untagged*	*Uncertain*
A	22	13	2
B	4	1	2
C	–	–	–
D	2	–	–
TOTAL	28	14	4

Other wildlife—saw a deer by Stream B, the first we've seen in the lower elevations in forest; saw a great blue heron by weir again; continued to see small flocks of ducks.

October 15

10 A.M. water level 79 centimeters
10 A.M. water temp. 46 degrees F

Weather: mostly sunny with cumulus clouds on horizon. By twilight, sky was perfectly clear.

We took advantage of gorgeous fall weather while it lasted and set off on another, maybe the last, of our long hikes in the high country. We climbed the twin mountains (els. 2,235 feet and 2,473 feet) about 3 miles north of the lake, which serve as its backdrop viewed from the lake's south end. We then descended to the nameless lake at 920 feet elevation southeast of "Pinnacle Peak." Returned to Ford Arm Lake from it by another route. A long, punishing day, tough on the knees; we made it back to the lake by Stream D after a painful descent in forest quickly filling with darkness. Saw only 2 deer all day.

Our ascent was via Stream D, and we found 2 dead cohos—one tagged, the other not (and with no sign of a tag hole). The tagged fish had come through the weir in August. It was lying maybe only 50 yards from the lake.

The untagged fish was at least one-half mile from the lake, marooned in a dry streambed. Perhaps it was lured up in the floodwaters and then left high and dry when they retreated. Stream D still only flows for about 250 yards above the lake before disappearing beneath its thick gravel deposits. For about the next one-half mile or so it is dry, except for unconnected small pools.

October 16
                              noon water level 73 centimeters
                              noon water temp. 45 degrees F

Weather: a frosty, clear day; frost on grass & weir until sun melted it in afternoon. Won't be long now till the snow flies . . .

No weir activity today, except that at about noon I caught a young, blackish bear trying to climb over our fence at this end of the weir (same section damaged previously by bears). When I appeared and shouted "Hey! What's going on here?" he snorted an answer I didn't catch and bolted over to a rusty-colored companion 30 yards away in the woods that I hadn't seen before. The two of them, and possibly a third, stampeded away through the brush. They appeared small; perhaps 2- or 3-year-olds? Siblings?

We walked to saltwater today. No sign of spawning activity by cohos in the 250 yards between weir and the waiting pool. At the pool there were easily more than 100, though continuing turbidity prohibits seeing any fish more than a foot or two below the surface.

October 17
                              11 A.M. water level 70 centimeters
                              5 P.M. water level 75 centimeters
                              11 A.M. water temp. 43.5 degrees F

Weather: overcast with gentle rain all day

I left the cabin only to clean the weir, get temperature and water level readings, and hit the outhouse. A day to rest the knees, read, think long thoughts, and savor the solitude.

Last night a bear was nosing around the front yard. Sometime today between my morning and evening visits to the weir I found our fence trampled over again in one place. I've decided to stop hoping they (the bears) will learn their manners—I undid this section and rolled it back so they can walk through unhindered. Next flood we will simply have to put it back together—all of a 5-minute operation.

October 18   *11 A.M. water level 101 centimeters*
                                 11 A.M. water temp. 45 degrees F

Weather: overcast with low ceiling; some light rain

Managed to coax a few cohos (26) into the trap today. Yesterday's light rain was only enough to raise the water by about 30 centimeters at most.

Started out with dip-net to check inlet stream B, the big one, this afternoon. The water level was moderately high, which probably contributed to the difficulty of seeing cohos. We only made it about 40% of the way, because this stream requires a lot of attention. Even searching more thoroughly than we did 4 days ago, we dug up only 10 cohos.

On our return at dusk, we saw the "regular" brown bear at the far end of the weir (near trap). To see how he would react, I tried pumping a shell from the magazine into the chamber of the 12-gauge. To our delight and satisfaction, he moved swiftly away immediately upon hearing that metallic racket. To him it signaled that he was about to be stung, although I had no intention of doing so, provided the bluff worked. Amazing, it only took one penalty and he is already conditioned. That's got to be faster than Pavlov's dogs learned!

I think there's a very good chance that if it hadn't been for this negative conditioning, we would have had some kind of confrontation by now . . . and either he or we would be *much* the worse for it.

*

October 18, 1982
Monday

Dear Folks,

Well, I've put in seventy days here now, at least seventy percent of my total stay. It has really gone by fast. It's a rare moment that I feel bored or wish that it were all over. I am contented here now that things are pretty well under control. Perhaps "pretty well under control" is not right. The weather always has something up its sleeve, and our gadgetry firmly follows the laws of entropy (i.e., it breaks down a lot!).

Radios in particular have been a real nuisance. They've had to ship in a different one to us with each food drop, because something always goes wrong. The first blew a fuse in the transmitter. The second was off-frequency. The third refused to switch on after the leads sparked when I was disconnecting the battery. And so on. Once we went for almost two straight weeks out of total contact with the outside world. I began to worry just a little that maybe the outside world was no longer there; certainly the omnipresent gray clouds gave me no reassurance.

At other times we are able to hear but not be heard. This is even more frustrating.

— "Calling KE-6628 Ford Arm Lake, KWB-353 Juneau."
— "Ford Arm back to Juneau." pause . . .
— "KE-6628 Ford Arm Lake, KWB-353 Juneau."
— "Ford Arm to Juneau, go ahead!" pause . . .
— "Juneau clear of Ford Arm Lake, no contact . . ."

On the special occasions when the radio does work, it's fun to listen into the Fish and Game conversations between 8:00 and 9:00 A.M. We can receive from all over southeast Alaska: Ketchikan, Petersburg, Sitka, Haines, Chilkat Lake, Politofski Lake, Stikine River, etc., plus various boats. You get to hear whether the weather elsewhere is as miserable, what flying conditions are, fish counts, food lists, and other business that really doesn't interest anyone but Fish and Game employees in the bush.

In one of my earlier letters I mentioned that I was enamored of the voice of a woman who worked at the Chilkoot weir. I don't hear her anymore, so I think that operation has shut down for the season. But no matter. Now I'm in love with the voice of one of the secretaries in the Fish and Game office in Petersburg. What a doll! Every time I hear her good-natured "Roger, Roger!" I sigh. Detlef grins and just shakes his head. At the same time, I'm quite happy that I'll probably never meet her in person. I doubt if she'd ever be able to live up to that sexy voice.

We have had a couple of October floods now. One rose just high enough that we could admit herds of cohos into the trap and pass them upstream. We tagged over 250 fish in just two days, one-fourth of the season's total.

The other flood came on the heels of the first and nearly canceled out our weir. One day it rained steadily from noon on, but by darkfall the water level still hadn't climbed enough to make us wary. Still the rain poured down on us.

By midnight I was getting concerned and checking the water level against the weir every hour. Then, when I went out to check at 1:30 A.M., I nearly fell over at how suddenly the water had risen. It was above the banks and pouring over the top of chicken wire I'd attached to the top of the weir. Debris (sticks, fallen leaves, and needles) was piling up against the weir and plastering it so water couldn't get through, forcing it to go over.

Our precarious catwalk atop the weir was under water, making the traverse across the weir trickier than normal. It was a desperate night with no time even for a wink of sleep—I was emotionally "wired"; couldn't have slept anyway; it was reminiscent of all too many all-nighters as an undergraduate. At least this time I wasn't worried about completing an assignment on time; it was just a matter of holding the fort. Nor did I have to think any more creatively than what it took to pull leaves out from chicken wire.

By the gray light of dawn, the weir looked like a besieged fort, or a battle-field. It was plastered with debris, half-eaten fish (bears again), and topped by floppy rows of chicken wire resembling bales of barbed wire.

At 9:00 A.M. I managed to get through to Juneau and apprise them of our situation. I said I wasn't sure if we'd lost any fish. Moments later, I was quite sure. As I walked out to the weir, I saw fish escaping through a hole in fencing that connected to the weir on the side.

Then I saw cohos actually jumping over the weir in the center of the river! There the top of the chicken wire was only one or two feet above the water level, and one after another, fish catapulted themselves over it, some of them looking like Olympic high-jumpers the way they flopped and rolled over the wire. The scene triggered still more scurrying about in an effort to plug this escape route. Then it was time for some well-earned rest.

Love,
Leon

*

October 19   *11 A.M. water level 84.5 centimeters*
                               11 A.M. water temp. 46 degrees F

Weather: overcast & drizzling with occasional breaks in the cloud ceiling

Today we continued our walk up Stream B, pursuing it to the limit of salmon navigability. We did not probe under each undercut bank, as this would've consumed a full day or more. As Leon Shaul says, it seems probable that it is still a bit early yet; when the salmon move up en masse, we should have no trouble finding them.

We also walked Stream A, and though not as carefully as before, there still seemed to be fewer cohos than last week.

Detlef had a face-to-face encounter with a large dark bear. It occurred while I was exploring a tributary of Stream B and he started across the divide seeking me. As he was groping up a bank, all of a sudden a large furry head popped into view above him at the top of the bank. The bear reeled and walked off, grumbling loudly as it did. Detlef said it all happened so fast he had time for neither fear nor the gun. He believes the bear had come to investigate the source of noise, thinking perhaps he was another bear. Sounds like Detlef came within a whisker of experiencing an honest-to-goodness bear hug.

October 20   *10 A.M. water level 78.5 centimeters*
                               10 A.M. water temp. 45 degrees F

Weather: overcast with occasional drizzles later in day

Not much of anything to report. No fish in trap. No action. Spent day writing, sketching, hiking up opposite slopes, reading, feeding, sleeping, defecating.

*

Dear Folks,

One of my daily rituals takes place almost without fail every dusk. I walk one of the bear paths over to the edge of the lake and stand there gazing on it quietly for a few moments. Then I lift my flute (recorder) to my lips and play some tunes that I'm fond of. I always finish with a pensive rendition of taps. It seems a fitting way to bid the day farewell.

At other times I grab the flute and take the raft out to the center of the lake. There I cut the motor and just drift, savoring the pristine panorama and allowing the vast silence to seep into my soul. I detect a presence then, palpable, but beyond the reach of my comprehension. Yet it fills my soul with an ineffable ecstasy. My heart is soothed by a deep sense of harmony that can only come from touching something beyond ourselves. Goose bumps erupt on my arms.

Fingering the little flute, I play "Ode to Joy" from Beethoven's Ninth Symphony. Recorders can sound shrill and childish, about as serene as a kazoo. But here somehow, the notes are transformed into sublime, transcendental music, which resonates and echoes beautifully in the enormous natural amphitheater around me. And I feel a kinship then, across time and space, from the Alps to the Andes, with everyone who has ever been inspired to song by a natural setting or wondrous mountains climbing into God's heavens.

Back to the radio. Oftentimes we cannot be heard clearly in Juneau while we can "copy" them just fine here. Then, the voice may say something like, "Did you say one thousand twenty-one adult unmarked cohos? Is that a Roger?" To which I will reply "Roger, Roger!" My partner and I got, and still get, a kick out of the way these folks have their own radio lingo. I guess "Roger" is used far more widely than just in Alaska Department of Fish and Game circles though.

At first I wondered why people don't just say "yes" instead. It seemed like saying "Roger" all the time was like all those silly people saying "ten-four" during the CB radio craze a few years back—it's the "in" slang. I think now, though, that maybe "Roger" does have real utility when reception is very poor, because it's easy to make out with its two syllables and accent on the first; "yes," on the other hand, might be mistaken for a burp or some other meaningless sound.

Ma, you asked about food in one of your letters. We get virtually anything we want. Two days before I first came here I went grocery shopping in Juneau and had a total bill of five hundred dollars. Now we send food lists back on the food planes or give them over the radio. Fish and Game believes that allowing us to indulge in small creature comforts like food fetishes is fair compensation for the "tremendous privations" of these remote outposts. That's why I order two chocolate cakes on every food run!

We have a couple of large chests for frozen meats and fresh produce. We cook on a new three-burner Coleman stove. For baking we have a small collapsible oven that you stick right on top of the burner. So, the facilities are here to eat well, if not the will or the talent. Honestly though, I have improved immensely from those bleak days when a pot of unadorned bleached noodles was enough to satisfy me. I even do a little baking—chocolate cakes and chocolate chip cookies, of course. No peach pies though! I wouldn't dare to infringe on Granny's turf!

I am not getting nearly the reading or writing done I'd hoped to. Constantly having another person around means there's always a diversion. Right this moment Detlef asked me what kind of person my brother was. You can see how difficult it is to write you and describe Tom at the same time! Whenever I do try and isolate myself in reading or writing letters, which is not easy in a one-room fourteen-by-sixteen-foot cabin, Detlef feels shut out or ignored and it annoys him. He is neither the reader nor the writer that I am. Nor am I the card player he is. He brought a deck but all he ever gets to play is solitaire. Ah well, you have to expect these kinds of differences to produce a certain amount of friction under these cramped accommodations.

Several weeks ago we installed our Sears oil heater, so now we can laugh at the cold and the rain. It's so dreamy to come back to a cold cabin after a long, tiring hike or three hours in the drenching rain and be able to warm it up with the flick of a switch and the toss of a match; we have the pleasure of the wilderness without the pain. The spartan side of me sees the other side becoming soft as a grape, bourgeois, and decadent. The other side savors the comfort. The two sides will be battling till the end of my days.

Love,
Leon

*

October 21   *11 A.M. water level 84.5 centimeters*

                              11 A.M. water temp. 46 degrees F

Weather: high overcast with drizzle on and off; mountains dusted with first snow of the coming season

Detlef drew a map of the river from the weir to saltwater today, after pacing it carefully. The scale appears quite good considering he had no surveying equipment. He has tried to emphasize the various channels. He estimated about 300 salmon in the pool where they congregate.

In Detlef's walk, he bumped into a trio of bears (mother plus two large cubs?) who advanced to about 25 yards before detecting him, standing upright, and darting for cover. We also saw "the regular" bear just below the weir.

October 22   *noon water level 78 centimeters*

                              noon water temp. 44 degrees F

Weather: partly cloudy; little precip.

Today we hiked up the small tributary about ¼-mile below the weir shown entering the river from the south on the USGS quad. No sign of cohos there and doesn't look like there will be—it's too small and steep. We climbed to above timberline after thrashing through some incredibly treacherous, thick alders clinging to a steep slope. One slip of a grip for either of us would've proved very nasty. The chin-ups we do every day on our makeshift chinning bar back in camp paid off handsomely. (Getting the shotgun up through this thicket was a test of patience! The barrel kept getting snagged.)

In the alpine meadows, our feet tasted the first wet snow of a new season. For a while we were whited out and flurried on; then the clouds fled to reveal stunning views of mist-draped mountains crowned with fresh snow. We saw 2–3 deer near timberline.

*

October 22, 1982
Friday

Dear Folks,

Here are a couple of picturesque descriptions of Juneau in the eyes of the capital-move proponents in the early 1960s:

> "a teeny-weeny polka dot city . . . hardly more than a toehold on earth, squeezed between rugged mountains. . . . A man can walk a half-mile south from the Baranof Hotel, in the heart of the downtown district, to the end of civilization."

> "residence in the isolation of Juneau, and the daily routine there, has a psychological effect on employees which is detrimental to the State government in general. . . . Large trucks are an oddity. Cars with out-of-state license plates are seldom seen. . . . I have often had the feeling that this huge state is governed from a kind of lost colony of Atlantis, an almost unreal city shrouded in mists and reached only after an uncertain journey."

Now, in just a couple of weeks, Alaska voters will be deciding Juneau's fate when they cast their votes in the capital-move referendum. Before I left town, statewide polls indicated that the electorate would vote to move the capital, that is, approve the billion-dollar-plus price tag. In a way I'm sorry not to be in Juneau now, because I'm sure it's on everyone's mind. It must be kind of strange for people who really call Juneau home to know that its fate will be determined not by its own residents, but by the residents of Anchorage, over five hundred miles away, for Anchorage has half the votes in the state. But that's the price of depending on the purse and the whims of the public. (The entire point of the initiative is to move the state capital within easier reach of the bulk of its population, and thereby theoretically make government more accountable. "Willow" is the name of the potential new capital site, a short distance north of Anchorage. Except for a few homesteader types, I think its only inhabitants are real estate speculators!)

I guess I tend to oppose the move, mostly because of the blow it will be to Juneau. Unfortunately, if Juneau remains the capital, the boosters and boomers will ensure that eventually it will grow too big to be considered a rustic frontier town anymore. And with the corresponding increase in pilots, boaters, hunters, and fishermen, it'll be that much harder to find empty, unspoiled places in southeast Alaska. McDonald's just arrived in town last year, prompting me to write a letter to the *Juneau Empire* (daily newspaper) observing wistfully that when Ronald McDonald arrives in town, and the "sign of the golden arch" (i.e., trash) is visible everywhere, you know "the last frontier" has passed on.

Well, winter is fast on its way. Already the first fleets of snow flurries have arrived, sprinkling the surrounding mountaintops. They look so much more majestic, in a cold, cruel way, wearing their crowns of white. The snow accents each crag and sharpens every line.

Detlef and I climbed up to timberline on a ridge beside a ravine. For a while a cloud locked in on us and it flurried. Then as suddenly as the cloud gathered, it dissipated, revealing stunning vistas of a landscape in transition from one season to the next. The westering sun was shimmering on the surface of the frigid Gulf of Alaska, creating an illusion of inviting tropical waters.

On our descent, once again in the forest, we paused frequently to admire the intense green hue of the mosses where soft, golden shafts of the setting sun came to rest. At another moment, we beheld a sun shower glittering in the ethereal evening light.

It's nice to behold the pageant of nature unfolding at its own pace, without the distraction of trips to town. I arrived in the summer, and now it's almost winter.

The pinks, chum, and sockeye salmon have come and gone, and now the cohos are well into their last rites. The migrating waterfowl pass overhead daily, and some stop for the night at the lake. I am witness to nature's eternal rhythms . . . I have never asked for more out of this life.

Love,
Leon

*

October 23

noon water level 72.5 centimeters

noon water temp. 44 degrees F

Weather: terrific gusts of wind began last night, shaking the tent like a rickety shell; these lasted until nearly afternoon, followed by hard but short-lived rain

An uneventful, ordinary day, but for the wind. One of the metal grommets on the tent fly was ripped off by its force.

We are getting restless again, waiting for hell to break loose and a flood of work to pour on us all at once.

Although we can barely get through on the dad-blamed radio, I think we were able to communicate that due to our ripped raft we would be unable to meet the floatplane in the middle of the lake next time. So we've arranged to place a cache of the stuff we're sending out on a large gravel bar at the outlet of one of the creeks into the lake. This afternoon I cached several items in a pile covered with a plastic sheet.

October 24

noon water level 76 centimeters

noon water temp. 43 degrees F

Weather: overcast with periods of rainfall

I've got bad news and worse news with regard to the cache we placed yesterday. First the bad news: the plane was supposed to come today but didn't. The worse news? A bear seems to have raided the cache last night. Although there was nothing that smelled of food, its curiosity drove it to "investigate" (i.e., rip apart) the cache anyway. A suitcase of mine, filled with books I was sending back to town, was ripped open. They all got soaked by the rain and have swollen up to twice or more their size. Sorry, Leon Shaul, but a book you lent me was among the damaged ones. Ironic, eh? It's a book about grizzly bears! At least it will have a story behind it as it sits all deformed up on your bookshelf.

I saw a most unusual little critter on the far stream bank 60 yards below the weir. It leapt about nimbly and nervously, and evinced a great curiosity in me as I stood watching from the stream. It had a very light gray head, shaped it seemed like a cat's, yet it had a thick bushy tail of almost orange fur, which no bobcat or lynx would have.

It would peer out at me from a crevice in the rocks. Then it would hop, with legs forward, to a rock where it sat on its haunches—as a dog or a cat would—and study me. With its tail it was maybe 2½ feet long. Its body was more darkly colored than the tail. Mink, marten, fisher, otter all came to mind, but I can't picture them sitting like a dog and I don't believe they have bushy tails. At this point my guess is a red or gray fox pup, but both of these are unsatisfactory for the simple reason that, according to my authoritative field guide, they don't even occur on these islands! I'm still baffled. (In hindsight, I am reasonably certain, but by no means positive, that this hyper little creature was a marten.)

I walked down to Ford Arm today. On my return from saltwater, I decided to take a bear trail that parallels the stream on the opposite side. We have used it before, and although we frequently saw large, fresh bear dung there we never saw any of the makers of the trail or the dung. Until today.

The gloom of evening was settling into the forest when I started up the trail. I rounded a boulder. There, looming 15 yards away, was the dark silhouette of a massive brown bear standing on two legs, facing me. It dropped to all fours, woofed, and bolted to my left into the obscurity. I shuddered and hastened on my own way.

As I neared camp, I saw another bear just 20 yards downstream from the weir, moving toward the cabin. But I saw no sign at all of him as I approached the cabin more closely. Phantoms of the Forest. I suspect that we have been uncomfortably close to bears much more often than we realize.

October 25

10 A.M. water level 85.5 centimeters
10 A.M. water temp. 43.5 degrees F

Weather: high, thin clouds A.M.; overcast and raining lightly much of P.M.

Food and mail (minus the mail!) drop today. Got several needed tools, like flashlights, dip-net, better radio, another raft. Called Juneau in P.M. and for the first time in ages, they could understand us clearly. Hope it lasts.

Reviewed instructions for mark-recapture sampling. They seem to make sense.

Immediately after talking to Leon on the ratio about our camp bears, we poked our heads out of the door to see one between us and the fuel barrels, walking toward the cabin. Of course, then we had to step outside to get a better look at it. When it caught wind of us, it actually loped *toward* us a few paces (prompting a mad dash on our part for the door!) before veering off toward the lake.

October 26

11 A.M. water level 88.7 centimeters

11 A.M. water temp. 43 degrees F

Weather: predominantly overcast with periodic squalls—wet snow & hail. Noon air temp. 37.5 degrees F.

The snow line dropped to about 1,500–1,600 feet overnight, the 1,720-foot mountain at the end of the lake being tipped with fresh snow. This is the coldest it's been so far on a cloudy day.

We spent a wearisome afternoon poking and probing under logs and banks in the 4 streams looking for spawning salmon. We caught only 2 the entire afternoon, not a very auspicious debut to our mark-recapture study. (Data on these two are in another notebook.)

As we motored toward the north end of the lake in the raft, we saw a couple of floating white objects near the entrance to Stream D. As soon as it was obvious they were birds, I cut the engine and took to oars. There were 2 very large white ones, and 3 smaller, grayer ones. They were well aware of us and took to the sky when we were still about 150 yards away. Without a doubt they were swans, presumably trumpeters. One of the adults honked anxiously a few times before they flew. They climbed, banked, and brought out the landing gear right away again for the descent into the small pond. The sight of them flying in formation against the whitened mountains is not one I'll easily forget.

When we returned to camp, Detlef discovered that 1 or 2 articles of clothing he'd left soaking in a washbasin in front of the cabin had been pulled out onto the ground. Hmm.

Later

After midnight; Detlef asleep. I stepped outside before hitting my bunk and the shadowy form of a bear went barreling away toward the weir. I followed. A minute later I saw a bear scale one of the tripods from behind and stand atop the catwalk. Now that's a climber! He walked swiftly away to the other end of the weir, grumbling. I was really rather unnerved to see him pop up from behind. Any sense of security I have felt looking down on bears while I stood on the weir was apparently false. It's not a barrier for them after all.

October 27   *11 A.M. water level 79.5 centimeters*
11 A.M. water temp. 41.5 degrees F
11 A.M. air temp. 32 degrees F

Weather: 1 inch of snow accumulated overnight; snow flurries on and off all day. A mostly cloudy day, but bright.

In the later afternoon I walked downstream to the braided portion of the river below the coho pool. Found 4–5 cohos spawning in the main channel there, all still quite lively. I also found one female coho, just dead, 20 yards downstream of the pool. She had breeding colors but looked thin and worn, spawned-out.

Saw a minklike creature traveling along opposite bank toward lake by weir A.M. (mink? marten? young otter?).

October 28   *10 A.M. water level 75 centimeters*
10 A.M. water temp. 41 degrees F

Weather: heavy overcast, light snow turning to light rain. In A.M. there was a total accumulation of about 3 inches of very fluffy snow.

It was a placid morning graced with gently falling snowflakes—large and fluffy. Most of the flakes were intercepted by needle and twig and never reached the ground under the trees.

Walked downstream in the afternoon. We spent about 15 minutes each independently estimating the number of cohos in the pool 250 yards below weir. Detlef's guess was "350 or less," mine "300 to 400." Below the pool we counted about 6 spawning, although this surely is an underestimate.

October 29   *11 A.M. water level 123 centimeters*
                                11 A.M. water temp. 43 degrees F

Weather: milder air temps., but heavily overcast all day with light rain much of P.M. Water level rising from dusk on.

Found a dead coho, #12031 (tagged October 9), washed against weir; looked depleted, spawned-out.

Got nearly 100 very ripe cohos through the weir today, thanks to a combination of rain last night and snowmelt.

We killed what I thought were to be our last 3 marked cohos today (to save heads to check for tag retention), but thanks to one of the furry rascals, we still need one more fish. I left a bucket containing the 3 fish beside the oil drums, near the water where we would remove the heads, while we retreated to the cabin to warm our icy hands first. I considered, but dismissed as unlikely in the middle of the afternoon, a bear raid on these choice morsels.

Again I must plead guilty to underestimating the opportunism of Mother Nature's children: half an hour later, I poked my head out the door in time to see a hairy posterior—one end of an enormous body, the other end of which was buried in our bucket. I shouted and rushed out. The bear was startled and ran, one juicy 11-pound fish dangling in its mouth. It couldn't have been too scared, though. Twice it paused to retrieve its prize when it dropped the fish. It loped into the brush headed downstream. Later Detlef explored down that way, but found nothing. Bears—1, Man—0.

October 30   *5 A.M. water level 156 centimeters*
                                1 P.M. water level 146 centimeters
                                1 P.M. water temp. 42 degrees F

Weather: good steady rain well into last night; overcast with sporadic hail & rain squalls A.M. & P.M.

Today we awoke to a trap full of fish more resembling packed sardines than spawning cohos. We quickly worked through them, not bothering with marks/scars for the first time, so as to clear the trap and admit more fish while the water remained high. This worked fairly well, and we did 163 fish today. That makes over 250 in 2 days, which should have made an appreciable dent in the population of stragglers below the weir. Numerous cohos are now spawning just upstream of the weir in the vicinity of our anchor system.

Bear at weir again this eve, as well as last eve (not in trap, but perches on pickets and dives for fish just in front of them). Also, saw what were probably the same 5 trumpeter swans yesterday and today. I have never seen another bird or beast so wary of people as these graceful creatures are. Approaching within a quarter-mile makes them visibly nervous. Are they so shy of us because of no prior experience with humanity—or too much?

October 31

noon water level 90 centimeters
noon water temp. 41.5 degrees F

Weather: generally overcast with a couple of short showers; water level falling

Today we went after spawning cohos in Stream A (and D for a few minutes). After all our previous fruitless trips, it was very satisfying to bag a number of the buggers. They are spawning in droves now; we netted 25 fish just in Stream A in about 3 hours' effort. There are probably at least three times that number in the stream currently. We did not have to resort to probing under banks and obstacles unless we saw the fish dart under them and it looked possible to drive them out.

The cohos were usually visible (though often protected by debris or logjams), so that we concentrated on sneaking up and pouncing on them, unsuspecting, with the net. We carried two dip-nets but not the seine; at this stage it seems we can catch enough fish without having to lug it around.

At day's end, of the fish we've recaptured, the tagged-to-untagged ratio (corrected for tag loss as best we can) stands at 24:7.

We have found Leon's instructions for mark/recapture sampling to be very useful, except for the part about standing on one's head and making a quick visual estimate of the number of fish in a pool. This requires more fisheries-biology training than either Detlef or I possess, so that it may be necessary to wait for one of our bosses to show us how.

The gurgling and splashing out in front of camp again—from the spawning cohos—are reminiscent of the bygone summer and sockeye season.

A flock of Canada geese just passed overhead in the moonlit sky—unseen but definitely heard. Their honking evokes the spirit of the wild better than any manmade music ever could.

*

October 31, 1982
Sunday

Dear Folks,

Somebody in Sitka blew it on the last plane flight here a week ago, so my mail is sitting there instead of here. Sure is a bumer when you *know* you've got mail and it's *such* a cure for loneliness.

We've begun the second and final phase of the project: "mark-recapture sampling." Since the overall objective is to obtain an accurate estimate of the "escapement," that is, the number of coho salmon that escaped being caught by fishermen to return and spawn; and since an unknown number got past our weir in the floods we've had, we now have to use a technique called mark-recapture sampling to arrive at an estimate of the overall escapement.

When the fish came through our weir we attached small tags to them. Now what we're doing is walking the four streams that flow into our lake. The cohos like to spawn on gravel beds in shallow water. There we net 'em up and check for the tags. This is a challenge. Actually, it's like a sport, which suits us both just fine, as former competitive athletes. (Note I did not say "has-beens!")

The tagged/untagged ratio can then be used to calculate, or get an estimate of, the escapement. Unfortunately, the pleasing simplicity of this technique is complicated by the fact that some fish lose their tags, that we didn't tag all the fish we counted at the weir, and that the tagged fish may have had a higher mortality rate because of our handling. Another possible factor is that the tagged fish may be more visible to predators like eagles and bears.

Anyway, it's fun to outsmart the fish and catch them, though more often than not they dart under an undercut bank or a log before we get the net on them. It's amazing to see such large fish in such small streams, some of them no larger than the brooks we can hop across on our land at Windy Ridge, West Virginia. The water is so shallow their backs actually stick out above.

Our nets are called dip-nets and they resemble tennis racquets in shape, although much bigger of course and made of aluminum and seine twine.

As you can guess, I'm reading a stack of books right now, but quite slowly. I just do not have all the free time I thought I would. One that I just finished is *Mutiny on the Bounty*, by Nordhoff and Hall. I read it in part because I was intrigued by what little I knew of the main character Fletcher Christian, ringleader of the mutineers, and whose name brother Tom sometimes uses when traveling incognito. The last paragraph of the book reads:

> The moon was bright overhead when I reembarked in the pinnace to return to my ship. A chill night breeze came whispering down from the depths of the valley, and suddenly the place was full of ghosts—shadows of men alive and dead—my own among them.

What a haunting passage!

I was intrigued to discover that the infamous (though perhaps maligned) captain of the HMS *Bounty*, William Bligh, was actually a junior officer some years earlier aboard one of Captain James Cook's voyages of exploration and discovery. It sailed along this very seacoast two centuries ago. The most venerable spruces near our cabin were also standing here back then, already large trees. If I were to count their growth rings I could find exactly which one corresponded to the year Cook and Bligh passed by.

Now when I am above timberline and peer out beyond the Myriad Islands to the Gulf of Alaska, across a view that is essentially unchanged from what it was two centuries ago, I can imagine the ghostly image of a tall-masted wooden sailing vessel, sails billowing in the salty breeze. In this setting, with so few distractions, the poignancy of *Mutiny on the Bounty* has pierced my heart. More than anything, I'll remember the tragic destinies of its characters (on whom it dawned, after the impulsive mutiny, that they could never return home again), the heartbreaking loss of loved ones, and the inexorable passing of people, places, and times, never to be recaptured.

Love,
Leon

*

November

November 1

Weather: overcast but no rain, except for slight drizzle around dusk

More mark-recapture sampling today. We walked about two-thirds the coho-navigable length of Stream B. Despite its length, size, width, and gorgeous gravel beds, this stream continues to be a disappointing producer compared to Stream A. We did get 30 fish examined, compared to 25 in Stream A yesterday, but it required 2 more hours of effort.

Part of the reason we get fewer fish per unit of stream length in Stream B is that it is chock-full of snags, roots, logjams, undercut banks, and anything else that hides fish or hinders us. Most of the fish also hang out in pools that are too deep to wade. Even considering these factors, I believe Stream B has a lower density of spawning cohos. It could be that it still hasn't shown us its major run yet.

Shagging cohos with our dip-nets is rapidly advancing into a science. As soon as we sight one potential victim, we can pretty well gauge our chances for success. We predict the likely escape route and move in with that in mind. Stalking these fish with nets is more fun than fishing with rod and reel (more action).

A number of times we have actually chased after escaping fish, sprinting 40 yards down the streambed through the shallows: a sort of "Feet vs. Fins" contest. It's exciting. But we won't set any world records running in chest waders through shin-deep water and over cobbles. And the footing is treacherous at best. I took a hard spill into the water once. Getting soaked was not as bad as banging my already-tender knee. I've been limping for several days.

November 2

2 P.M. water level 151 centimeters
5 P.M. water temp. 41.5 degrees F

Weather: dark & gray; rained steadily most of night, windy & drizzling most of day

Today we stayed at home and tended the trap, emptying it of eager cohos three times. Although there still are a number visible below the weir, they did not enter the trap very readily. We had to keep our eye on it so we could shut it before they all rushed out again.

Other than doing 105 cohos, not much else happened today. The bleak, lonely weather wore on me. For the first time I looked forward to leaving Ford Arm in a couple of weeks.

November 3

noon water level 100.5 centimeters
noon water temp. 41 degrees F

Weather: heavy overcast with gusts of wind and light rain

We went up streams D, C, and A (in that order) this afternoon. Stream D had perhaps 30 spawners that we saw (out of which we caught 15). All of the spawners were in about the first 150 yards of the stream, even though it was flowing above that point (which it does only during and after fairly heavy rain). We continued about 200 yards beyond the last fish we sighted before turning back, and onto happier hunting grounds.

We saw only 2 spawners in Stream C—both tagged and both upstream close to the pond, about where the forest gives way to muskeg. We couldn't catch them. Can't be too many more than this in Stream C, for it's small, short, and we poked under most banks, roots, and logs, to no avail.

Stream A was deep and swift today. We spent only about an hour along it and caught only 1 new fish. The deep water and swift current made it very difficult to operate.

Detlef found a jawbone lying right beside a floy tag (#12301) along Stream A, but we did not list this as a tagged fish because there is a chance the tag and the jaw didn't belong to each other.

*

Dear Folks,

Well, I can imagine that time is marching onward out in your world, dragging people and events with it. In here, in my small world, there is just the endless succession of uncounted, numberless days. There is little sense of a linear flow of time, with more recent events seeming closer and less recent events seeming more distant.

The weather changes from day to day, but except for the dwindling daylight and the snow line creeping down the mountainsides, there is nothing to mark the advancing seasons. No Halloween costumes and trick-or-treating. No ads for Thanksgiving turkeys or commercials announcing how many shopping days left before Christmas. Only our radio gives any meaning at all to the days of the week. We're supposed to contact Juneau or Sitka every workday, so this lends some structure, arbitrary as it is, to time. I usually know about what day of the month it is, because I keep the camp log. Otherwise, we would be lost in the depths of time.

Still though, we do live by the clock here, if our own clock. When the time was set back an hour several days ago, we kept our clock on daylight savings time, because we've gotten into the habit of rising so late that we couldn't afford to lose another hour of daylight in the evening. Now, we have advanced our clock two more hours, so that we are actually three hours off local time. I believe this gives us eastern standard time. This way, we can continue our slothful habit of starting the day at about noon and we will still have enough daylight to see what we're doing as we work outside. It won't get dark until 8:00 P.M.; on the other hand, it won't get light 'til 11:00 A.M.

Not long ago I talked with another weir operator, a fellow by the name of Larry Derby, whom I met in Juneau the week before coming out here. Larry is at Politofski Lake down on Baranof Island, about eighty miles south of here. We talk together on the radio about two nights a week, trading stories, advice, and consolation. Larry went through a divorce and fell in love again the week I met him, right before he disappeared into the bush for three months. Tonight he informed me that he'd just received a Dear John letter from his new love on the last mail flight.

Larry told me they have only had a third as many cohos through their weir as we have. They got one flood where they lost a lot of fish because the water rose four feet over the top of the weir. Matter of fact, it was two feet above the floor of the cabin. They'd lifted everything up to the loft and were ready to evacuate in their raft when the rains quit. Talking to Larry has made my headaches seem minor.

It's great to be able to communicate with a comrade across league after league of dark fjords and darker forests. The radio waves leap over mountain range after mountain range to a tiny outpost of civilization with two keepers huddled over their radio set. For a while, the lonely solitude retreats.

Sometimes we turn on our radio at about dusk, just to hear what we can. Often there is this strange, distorted music with an Oriental ring to it that rumor has it comes from Japanese fishing boats off in the Pacific. I don't know if I believe that, but I suppose it's plausible. We have also picked up the occasional shortwave broadcast from as far away as Africa, including one program called "Good Morning Capetown." Not much local news, I'm afraid.

I am still playing my recorder every day. Several times now, I have played within hearing range of brown bears. Unfortunately, they don't seem to react one way or another. I get neither boos nor applause. Guess they've never heard fine music before.

Love,
Leon

*

November 4   *1 P.M. water level 91 centimeters*
                               1 P.M. water temp. 41 degrees F

Weather: looked promising in morning but later clouded over; mild showers

The number of spawning cohos in inlet streams A and B seems to have plummeted almost overnight. On Stream A we saw only about 4–5 fish, down considerably from 4 days ago and even reduced from yesterday afternoon. In their place all we saw were numerous sets of jaws and remains of gills hauled up onto the banks and into the woods a few yards. The bears, eagles, and gulls seem to have done a very thorough job. In addition to the gills and jaws, innumerable bear turds lined the stream banks; it looked like a pasture full of cow pies out there. Either bears defecate that much more than cows or there is a veritable herd of grizzlies hidden in this forest.

In August, the bear scat was dark bluish with little blueberry seeds visible. It was in discrete mounds, like small logs. Now, as the bears' diet has shifted to salmon, their dung has become white and runny, forming pies instead of piles. It's strange to see the coho population being converted into bear meat and bear poop, an illustration of what ecologists refer to more academically as the "energy/matter transformations" in the food chain, all driven by the sun.

Stream B was not much better than Stream A. We broke one of the nets, so I returned to camp to rig up what I could. Detlef continued till dusk and was able to net 6 new fish by himself. This surge appears to be dying off. I sure hope it wasn't the main one, because we are still seeing far fewer fish than one would expect to see, given that we know there are 1,700-plus cohos in the system.

November 5

noon water level 79 centimeters
5 P.M. water temp. 40 degrees F

Weather: high overcast; gusty all day; no rain

It's weird—below the weir we seem to be getting an unaccountably large number of cohos; above it, in the spawning streams themselves, an unaccountably small number.

We checked again for spawning cohos below the weir today. While doing this we came upon the remains of 5 cohos—2 whole fish, 1 set of jaws, 1 backbone, 1 gill cover (all in different places).

November 6

noon water level 73 centimeters
noon water temp. 39 degrees F

Weather: clear, still, cool, sunny

We took advantage of the first really nice day in a while to hike up the last unclimbed mountain within our range—an unnamed 1,820-foot summit east of Stream B. It was a very pleasant, leisurely stroll up and down, in contrast to our rocketlike ascents and crash-and-burn, hell-bent-for-leather descents of previous hikes (which tend to trash the knees to shreds).

We attained awesome views of "The Proud Mountain"—el. 3,205 feet, with its pyramid summit and lower but sharper "crown" freshly arrayed in new snow. The north face is cruel and steep. Our ascent had been via the gentle, broad northwest ridge. Looking at the cold white summit pyramid today, it was hard to believe that not long ago I napped there.

We came across a rather unusual bear turd ¼-mile from Stream B. While it exhibited typical shape, size, and consistency, sticking cheerfully out of it was a little blue floy tag with the number 9304. It's almost as if the little tag was proudly announcing: "Look at me! I'm indestructible! A grizzly swallowed me but I'm still as good as new!"

I paused for a moment to ponder that since I had driven this tag into the fish it had passed through a brown bear's entire digestive tract, from mouth to anus! I felt like telling the tag: "Hey there, little trooper, your duty's done! We never expected you to mark dung as well!" I haven't decided yet whether to count this as a tagged fish in our mark/recovery survey. (The fish itself was rather difficult to reconstruct.)

Our dip-nets are nearly shot. Only 1 of the 4 is at all useful. Two hoops or rings have broken on us and two of the plastic connectors that join the metal loop to the handle have cracked and splintered. The heavy iron net is fine—because we never use it. It must weigh 10–15 pounds and is totally incapable of snaring a darting salmon. It might be useful for bear protection except that it is so hard to swing around—like swinging a loaded barbell.

So it was good that there were no fish visible in the stretches of either streams A or B that we walked. I hope the next rain will change that.

This morning we saw a bear print 2 feet from the base of the cabin steps. Detlef said he heard some snuffling very close just after I left the cabin to sleep in my dome tent.

November 7

1 P.M. water level 69.5 centimeters
1 P.M. water temp. 38 degrees F

Weather: clear, cool, sunny, little wind

Detlef walked downstream today. On his way down, he estimated 310 cohos. On his way back, he estimated 280. Suffice it to say there are still hundreds of cohos below the weir. These are *waiting*, not spawning cohos.

Detlef also scouted streams D and B and saw only 1 coho the entire afternoon, in Stream D.

Detlef slept in my 2-man tent last night and heard a bear kick up a fuss somewhere downstream. He thought maybe it was being chased (or vice versa), for the sound moved. I was in the cabin reading, and the torch (lantern) is so loud it would drown out a 5-megaton thermonuclear explosion at 300 meters, so I didn't hear the bear.

November 8

noon water level 67 centimeters
noon water temp. 37 degrees F

Weather: damp & overcast with periodic drizzling & snow flurries. Last night quite cool (below freezing). Note rapidly falling water temp. (6 degrees in last 1½ weeks).

Not much action today, except for my mouth and eyes (lots of talking and reading). Walked downstream and estimated about 350 cohos between here and pool. This is higher than both of Detlef's estimates yesterday (310 and 280). I am astonished at the crowds of fish still waiting to get past the weir. Word must've spread that we supply good drugs here (MS-222)!

Hiked a ways up the small tributary creek that enters our stream from the north ¼-mile downstream of weir. Saw a small deer; heard a motor on Ford Arm; heard too 6 shots fired in rapid succession. (First sign of any hunting here in over a month. Probably a resident from Sitka downcoast.)

November 9

10 A.M. water level 174 centimeters
5 P.M. water level 150 centimeters
5 P.M. water temp. 40 degrees F

Weather: rained steadily all night, more softly in morning, ceased in aft.; warmer; 11 P.M.—stars out

A very dark, dreary day; never got lighter than a dark shade of gray. It seemed to be either dawn or dusk all day long. Anyway, we did manage to tag 113 more cohos before they retreated. Nowadays, almost as soon as the water crests and begins falling off ever so slightly, they will not enter the trap in any large numbers.

Spoke to Dan Hutchins at Klakas Lake on Prince of Wales Island tonight. It was interesting to compare our circumstances.

November 10

noon water level 99 centimeters
noon water temp. 39 degrees F

Weather: cool and sunny, with thin, high film of clouds

Detlef walked downstream this morning. His most significant observation was that there were many more spawning fish than in previous visits.

We went coho-netting on Stream A and the upper part of Stream B today. Even handicapped as we were (with only one half-decent, patchy net and one very marginal, makeshift hybrid), we were much more successful in catching our quota today, attributable I suppose to our developing talent. Stream A did not have nearly the density of spawners as it did on October 31. Then we netted 25 there with much less bank-poking than necessary for today's haul of 9.

Stream B, on the other hand, or rather the limited reach of it that we covered today, was more densely populated than we've yet seen it, though not what I would call "crowded." It was still necessary to poke under many banks.

Finally got a glimpse of a few of the celebrities who have been leaving their autographs on the soft stream banks for us to gaze in awe at. As I emerged from a tangle of fallen trees on Stream A on our way up, I gasped at the sight of four chocolate brown bears 35 yards in front of me along the stream. They were equally startled, by the looks of it. Two stood briefly, woofed, and then they were all stampeding away from me toward Stream B, trampling over devil's club and grumbling in what seems to be typical bear fashion. The 4 consisted of a mother and 3 cubs about half her size. They all looked *big*.

We were returning to the boat along Stream A after dusk; too dim to distinguish colors any more. About 200 yards from the lake, suddenly there was a good-sized bear 25 yards in front of us, right in the stream. We stood riveted. Detlef reached for the gun slung over his shoulder, just in case. After 10 seconds or so, somehow the bear detected us and with a crash it was gone, to be followed seconds later by another bear about the same size. I'm pretty sure they were larger than the cubs, so in all probability, it was a 6-bear day . . . Make that a 7-bear day—just saw one at the weir!

*

November 11, 1982
Friday

Dear Folks,

Well, my time is running short. The project was *supposed* to terminate on November 15, but I haven't heard from my bosses in two weeks and there is no way we can pull everything together, saddle up, and be out of here in just four days.

Have I really been here three months? Only my daily log tells it must be so. All my intuition tells me is that I've been here for "a good while." In a way, this experience in social deprivation reminds me of a psychology experiment for which I once volunteered at the University of British Columbia. I received thirty dollars for it. For twenty-four nonstop hours I was isolated in a sensory deprivation chamber. It was utterly black, soundproof, with a small chemical toilet, a bed to lie on, and two tubes. One tube contained water, the other Metra-cal, a protein drink. In this dark chamber I underwent an intense experience of self-scrutiny and emotional recollections. My dreams were so vivid I lost the ability to distinguish between dream reality and waking reality. I wanted so much to talk to someone and describe what I was undergoing, but there was no one.

Likewise here. I think I'll be every bit as bubbly and expansive when I return to town as I was when I left that isolation chamber for the broad light of day. It will be weird to observe other faces and other people. I know that when I see our pilot every few weeks, I'm struck by his clean-shaven face. Of course, I haven't shaved, or showered for that matter, since early August. You can really begin to see how astonished North American Indian tribes must have been when that first tall-masted sailing ship carrying white men and so many new technological marvels appeared on the horizon.

Several nights ago I was curled up in my sleeping bag on my bunk, reading, when from outside there came the sound of so much slurping, snorting, crunching, and grunting that I was sure a garrison of grizzlies had set up camp beside ours. Never one to let good sense prevail over curiosity, I stepped outside cautiously with flashlight and shotgun, wearing only my long johns. While the sounds persisted, I couldn't see anything. This surprised me, because I thought a family of bears was out and about, and while a bear in the brush may not be as conspicuous as an elephant strolling down Madison Avenue, it should still stand out more than a mouse in a hayloft. After standing for nearly 10 minutes out there, leg muscles quivering in the cold, I still hadn't seen anything.

Then I caught sight of a long, slender, sleek animal on a rock in the lake — obviously not a bear! My question was answered. It was an otter — no, three of them. They were merely passing through town. And what table manners! Their uncouth vocalizations would have given poor Emily Post a heart attack. I don't think they chew with their mouths shut! But they seem to enjoy themselves; otters are noted fun-lovers. It's said they construct mud slides and skid down them again and again for the sheer fun of it. They are related to minks, skunks, ferrets, weasels, and wolverines (members of the weasel family, or Mustelidae, with malodorous glands) but not to beavers or seals. Eventually the 3 "mustakeers" slid boisterously on into the night, and I, teeth chattering, climbed back into my chilled sleeping bag.

A couple of weeks ago I saw a critter the identity of which baffled me — only seventy-five yards from camp. Was it just passing through on an unknown mission, or does it live close by and make some of the strange night sounds we have occasionally heard?

I thought I would tell you more about Detlef. I have lived through high and low water with him — literally — for almost three months now, as opposed to only three weeks with Dan. Detlef and I have gotten under each other's skin, and into each other's hearts, far more than Dan and I had time to. I dare say that no married couple ever learned more about each other than we have in these months, unless both were unemployed as well as totally severed from contact with all other people—as we have been. What a psychological laboratory!

Speaking of marriage, I don't know if I'd already mentioned, but Detlef is married to an American he met while she was a foreign exchange student in Germany. They wed over there a few years ago, then moved back to The States (New York), and finally to Alaska, in this past year. It has not been a smooth marriage, apparently. In fact, Detlef had hoped that this three-month separation would give them the time and space to sort things out and renew their appreciation for each other. You know—"absence makes the heart grow fonder." For him at least, it seems to have worked. He is forever expressing tender thoughts for his wife. I think that's the result of three months of listening to my wistful reminiscences and regrets about my failed relationship with Vicki last year in Canada. I constantly rue the fact that I didn't feel a sense of commitment toward her until it was too late.

As I try to describe Detlef's personality in general, with a few choice words, I stall out, unable to make any categorical statement without a disclaimer. I can't stuff him into a nutshell; he's too rich, complex, deep, contradictory. Thus while he laughs a lot and believes in not taking life too seriously, he can become morose about personal business and public affairs, brooding hard and long. While he advocates tolerance, he can be quite intolerant of what he sees as intolerance. While, like many West German youths, he is very antiauthoritarian or anarchic in principle, he berates his fellows for what he sees as their inconsistencies and hypocrisy.

For example, he rather disdains the participants in mass antinuclear rallies in Europe, which surprises me. On the other hand, he had refused service in the German military on moral and pacifist grounds. (As an alternative to military service, he had to work in an abortion clinic, where he saw countless bloody aborted fetuses; so now he is both pro-choice and pro-life). Based on his general outlook on life, I'd have thought Detlef would be spiritual kin to the antinuke demonstrators. And I reckon he is, except that he holds a massive distrust of any group psychology or mob rule.

Detlef believes ardently that any time an individual joins a group, he compromises his moral or intellectual principles. He is a firm believer in the rights and responsibilities of the individual. In many a discussion he has voiced his fear and loathing of the herding instincts, fears, and bigotry that a Hitler could capitalize on to mesmerize and later enslave a people, leading to atrocities against scapegoats like the Jews, and eventually to complete autoannihilation.

Detlef would be tagged "left wing," according to orthodox labeling, but this would be at least partly misleading. He once told me that he is "half-hippie, half-fascist." He greatly dislikes the regimentation of life in Communist East Germany from what he knows of it, and the horrendous propaganda pouring out of that country's government. He is convinced that many of East Germany's leaders are unreformed, unpunished, opportunistic war criminals.

Detlef is a sentimentalist and traditionalist — liking older-style clothing, proclaiming an interest in listening to elders and a strong belief that they deserve more respect than they now receive, revering workmanship and time-honored skills. He showed me a beautifully crafted leather quiver he had fashioned for his arrows. He made his own arrows, and every night in camp he diligently pulls his ninety-pound longbow, building up strength and poise for the day he hopes to hunt deer with it. You have to be strong enough to hold the arrow pulled back and take careful aim without your arm beginning to shake. Detlef believes in living simply and close to nature. The inability to do so in contemporary Germany was one reason he wanted out. It's too populated and too technological.

He wears his hair long, often in a bun, but he is by no stretch of the imagination a hippie or "flower-child." He drinks alcohol infrequently and abhors any other mind-altering drugs, even one as mild as marijuana. One German friend's increasing use of grass was a major factor in their growing apart.

Detlef has one of the softest voices I've ever heard in a man. Deceptively soft. And although his youthful face, long blond hair, and slender frame make him look delicate, the observer who thought this would be severely miscalculating. In body and spirit, on the scale from pansy to blade of steel, he stands far closer to the blade. By tying a round metal tube between two trees, we made ourselves a chinning bar, which we both use daily.

A long-time soccer player, Detlef has all my stamina and then some maybe. Anybody who can pull a ninety-pound bow and hold it taut for five or ten seconds is no weakling. He is a consummate fisherman, able to cast a line fifty yards and plop a lure into an area the size of a fish's mouth. He delights in mastering skills involving motion and finesse.

In his native Hamburg, Detlef joined a fishing club, which he said was about the only way to get access to fishable waters in northern Germany. The "fishable waters" were drainage ditches and the only fish were carp. He patiently stalked his prey in the murky ditch water and was elated when after hours of effort he would catch a strapping six-inch carp. And inedible at that! (Too much junk in the water.)

When Detlef first landed at Ford Arm and saw thirty-inch, fifteen-pound cohos mingling by the hundreds in a pool below the weir, he thought he'd reached an angler's paradise. At his first opportunity, he headed downstream with a couple of his rods and tackle. I didn't see him till the end of the day.

He looked distraught. "Didn't you catch anything?" I asked. "Are you kidding?" he answered vigorously, "I have never caught so many fish in my life, or ever been so bored by it! It was impossible not to catch them. They were so thick that even if no fish grabbed the lure, the hook would snag another fish in the back. There was no challenge at all. It's not the thrill I expected." And that was the last fishing he did, pretty much.

Detlef has at least the level of appreciation for the wilderness that I have. He is very sensitive not only to its visual beauty but to its changing moods. He often amazes me at how verbally expressive he can be in a foreign tongue. He is also an artist. On some high hilltop he will sit down and sketch a view of a lake, filling in the details later, back in camp. His real specialty, though, is fish, and his renderings in watercolor are quite good. He is so meticulous and painstaking. After outlining the fish and sketching in the broad features, he fills it in scale by scale.

Detlef's appreciation for the artistic beauty of fish is so transcendent that he can be oblivious to all else. Various times while we were tagging fish together he would stop and admire a particularly handsome specimen. Holding it up, he would rotate it and examine it from different angles, as if it were a model, all the while complimenting it for its striking colors, pronounced snout, or impressive size. "Oh you are a sexy one!" he would say. "All the lady fish will want you to fertilize their eggs!"

Now I too admire fish, but after standing for four hours in forty-degree water and nonstop rain, my ability to feel that admiration was muted to say the least! With stiff, wrinkled hands and feeling damp all over, all I wanted to do was finish work and retreat to a warm, dry cabin. Detlef, while undoubtedly as cold and wet as I, could still pause to savor a fish's beauty in these circumstances.

We have a song that we hum, whistle, or sing to make light of the miserable weather. It's an old tune by the Beatles, and the words go: "When the rain comes, they run and hide their heads; they might as well be dead." As near as I can tell, the lyrics poke fun at people addicted to dreary comfort, control, and routine in their lives. Like zombies, they are unable to tolerate—much less exult in—anything out of the ordinary bombarding their senses, like a few raindrops disrupting their carefully designed, delicate hairdos. So we croon these lyrics to remind ourselves of how hardy we are by comparison, facing the rain and even enjoying it sometimes, day after day. It boosts sodden spirits.

Detlef is also something of a cartoonist; humorous drawings sprinkle the pages of his own journal. I have always received a queer, ineffable, very pleasurable sensation just being in the presence of someone engaged intently or creatively in a task, and when Detlef draws or plays tunes on his harmonica, I feel this way.

From this description you can see what an intriguing person Detlef is, but it is still all but impossible to be sure whether or not he and I would be compatible in the bush together. As it turns out, I think we are—we're both still alive and on speaking terms—but it has still been a bit bizarre. Sometimes, more than a bit bizarre.

Twice we have gotten into heavy discussions, being as frank as we dared in revealing our impressions of each other. Twice, I told Detlef that I like him a lot, generally enjoy his company, thought that whatever friction I do feel was inevitable due to the cramped circumstances, and that, in sum, I thought our friendship would continue beyond our forced confinement together.

In turn, twice he told me that he didn't think we had much in common, that although he couldn't really say anything too bad about me to anyone, nor could he say that I was very special either, and that, in sum, he didn't think our friendship would last and that it took him by surprise that I did. Talk about diametrically opposed views of reality! And there is no neutral third party here to turn to for their opinion. Am I nuts, is he nuts, or are both of us bananas?

Detlef is a very astute observer of behavior and relationships. For instance, he commented once on how interesting it was that we had each slipped into our own roles—I always ran the outboard motor, he always netted and handled the fish, I always took the notes, etc. He wondered if these routines had become so ingrained in such a short time that we had lost some of our flexibility and freedom. If he walked up and took over the outboard motor on one of our trips across the lake, for example, without asking me, would I become miffed at his invasion of my "territory"? I have to admit I would. Controlling the outboard was part of my identity. We were not unlike a married couple where without question the man sits in the driver's seat when they both get into a car.

In spite of his acumen, however, it seems to me that Detlef frequently misinterprets others' conduct because of a disturbing tendency he has to read the worst possible motives into it. This is a human failing that is quite common of course, and one that touches all of us to some degree, at one time or another. Including me.

Detlef cooks dinner most of the time, since I am usually busy with my record-keeping duties as weir supervisor in the evening. When the meal is ready, with a flourish he always serves me my portion as if he were a waiter. Just before we chow down, he wishes me a robust "Bon appétit!"

In contrast, whenever I prepare the meal, I simply leave Detlef's portion right in the pan for him to get himself. I serve myself and start eating, immersed in a book usually. Detlef called this to my attention as an example of how cold and aloof I can be. It hurt him that I didn't go to that extra bit of trouble to serve him his plate and make him feel special.

In turn, his observation stung me because I realized he had a point. I can be oblivious to the little gestures of friendship and affection that we human beings delight in. Two years ago for my birthday, my Canadian girlfriend sewed me a shirt, bought me a Swiss Army knife, and treated me to dinner at an expensive restaurant. How did I mark the occasion of her birthday? I forgot it.

Detlef and I sleep in a bunkbed built of four-by-eight-foot sheets of plywood and two-by-fours. I sleep on top; he volunteered for the bottom, which has so little head space it is more like a slot than a proper bunk. You can't sit up without bumping your head and you have to slide into it carefully. Detlef enjoyed penciling graffiti onto the bottom of the upper bunk inches above his head. One of the messages read "I'm going crazy!" We thought it would be funny for our boss Phil to come out and read, but maybe it wasn't entirely a joke.

Detlef always went to bed an hour or two before I did. I would stay up reading by lantern light, first in a makeshift easy chair built of plywood and then in my bunk above his. Yet in spite of his earlier bedtime, Detlef surprised me at how late he would sleep in the morning. On days when there wasn't urgent work to be done or a long hike to take, 11:00 A.M. or noon wasn't uncommon. He was apparently sleeping some ten to twelve hours daily. "That's odd that a young, energetic guy needs so much sleep," I thought to myself. Then one night I found out why.

He had hit the bunk, per custom, an hour before. I climbed up into mine and brought the lantern, which I hung on a nail so I could read for a few more minutes. The lantern cast a homey yellow glow about the cabin interior and burned with a low hiss. The air was chilly, because I'd turned off the oil heater. I wore a wool cap and I could see my breath.

I had been reading in a sleepy daze for about ten minutes when all of a sudden I was startled by a plaintive voice from the dead zone below. "Leon, don't you care that I can't sleep?" asked Detlef. "Jeez, I'm sorry," I blurted out, "I didn't realize I was keepin' ya up. I'll turn out the lantern if that's what's bothering you."

"The lantern isn't what's bothering me. What bothers me is that you don't care that you keep me awake at night." I was dumbfounded; I didn't know what to say. "OK, Detlef, OK, I care. Believe me, I care," I pleaded. And that's how we entered a long discussion in which I learned that, outward appearance to the contrary, Detlef was usually not asleep during my long hours awake reading. The light and noise of the lantern and my every movement disturbed him. My lack of awareness perturbed him probably even more. Then, moments after I would douse the light, he would hear my snoring and get even more annoyed, which prevented him from falling asleep for yet another while.

"Damn, Detlef, why didn't you ever tell me that my being up and moving around disturbed you?" I asked. "I wouldn't have kept doing it all this time if I knew it bugged you." And Detlef answered me with a question of his own: "Why didn't you ever think of asking if it bothered me?" It was a standoff. But from that point on, we had an understanding. If I was going to stay up reading for a while, either he or I would retreat to one of the nylon dome tents, which we set up outside again.

Detlef had a point—I could be oblivious. But where he went wrong was in believing that I deliberately ignored his rights and needs. Yet I could be almost totally self-absorbed, as revealed on another occasion. One evening I was reading in my easy chair while Detlef was practicing with his longbow, pulling it from all sorts of positions. I could see him out of the corner of my eye. At one point I heard a slight snap and Detlef huff, but I didn't look up because I was engrossed in my reading.

Several minutes later, I heard Detlef ask, "Leon, do you know what just happened?" "What? Eh?" I stammered as I looked over and saw him sitting on the edge of his bunk staring intently at me. "You didn't even notice, did you?" "Notice what?" I blurted testily. He nodded to himself, as if confirming something. "My bow broke," he said sadly. His beloved custom-made longbow had snapped in half. Even though he practiced pulling it nightly, he had actually shot only a single arrow with it ever. The bow didn't come cheap either, not to a college student like Detlef.

I gave him my condolences, but he seemed disappointed in my character regardless: I hadn't even noticed his setback. "Well, it hardly made any noise and you were so quiet about it, how was I supposed to notice?" I attempted in vain to defend myself.

Incidents like these aside, however, we have really gotten on quite well together. We've shared many a chuckle; raw, wet hands; a lot of panting on steep ascents; and numerous discoveries. I'm extremely fortunate to be with someone who is perceptive and who, like me, feels a sense of awe at the natural wonderland that surrounds us.

We have been on some marvelous hikes together. Whenever we are about to head for the hills, I invoke the inspiring memory of the pioneering conservationist/naturalist/explorer John Muir. Revered by those who remember him (reviled by many in his time), Muir was a tireless, fearless explorer. I tell Detlef of how he would begin a multiday solo trip into wild mountain ranges and glaciers with nothing but crackers to eat and a wool blanket to sleep under. No Goretex rain gear, no plastic jugs of Kool-Aid, no freeze-dried food or cozy sleeping bags and lightweight nylon tents. His feats make our hikes seem like comfortable strolls by comparison.

Other times, tent-bound, Detlef and I amused ourselves ridiculing ads on the backs of cereal boxes and in magazines. "Can't pinch an inch!" proudly declared a tennis player to his anorexic wife on one brand of cereal billing itself as low-calorie. Her beaming expression said it all: "I exist to please you!" A magazine ad for a luxury auto showing two handsome businessmen dressed for success was just as telling and ludicrous a commentary on the "self-worth equals net worth" philosophy that permeates our culture.

It was nice to be with someone who, as I did, saw the humor, the humanity, and the vanity in all this.

I know that I will remember Detlef Büttner and Dan Hutchins as long as my memory functions at all. They are certainly memorable characters. And buddies. (Whatever they may think!)

I have continued to see bears regularly, sometimes at closer than "preferred" range. Near as I can tell, the closest one ever came to me was about ten yards. For a while we had one brown bear that visited the weir every day, sometimes standing or sitting on the bank watching us with envy as we tagged salmon in the trap. Once or twice he became too eager and looked as if he was about to start across the slippery fifteen yards or so that separated us, so he could help with the fish! But what he had in mind for the fish was not what we did.

We became uneasy and fetched the shotgun in the cabin, shell in chamber, in case he should try anything not-so-funny. We never had to use the gun at such short range, but having it there gave us confidence, so that we could keep him away by loud noise and bold gestures. Detlef threw rocks, which seemed to confuse and scare him.

It was fascinating to watch his behavior and his facial expressions and his reactions to various stimuli. Although my interpretation is probably only partially right, I had the distinct impression that as he watched us, sorely desiring the fat fish we handled, he was like a big but immature dog that could be dangerous because he had so much to learn about the "pecking order" of the world. What made us go for the shotgun is that his hunger seemed to be on the verge of overcoming his fear of the unknown (us).

We had received instructions on driving away problem bears through the application of a dose of birdshot to their posteriors from a safe distance; that is, shooting them in the rear with a load of light pellets, enough to frighten and sting, but not to wound or blind.

Well, one day I decided it was time we taught this bear a lesson. He'd already grabbed and eaten one of the salmon we had just tagged and released before it had time to recover from the anesthetic. For once, conditions were perfect—he was in full view, he was walking away, and he was about forty yards off. I took aim and fired. The gun flashed with a nearly deafening *BOOM* that reverberated through the gap.

The bear jumped like he had been nipped, and charged up the hill, but only about twenty-five yards before sitting down to nurse his fright, or perhaps the sting in his fat fanny. Five minutes later we were in the trap and he was eyeing us as enviously as ever! That doesn't quite sound like "never to return" to me.

Oh well, that's when we retreated from the machine age to the stone age and just tossed a few rocks at him. It looked like he was starting to realize that maybe we should be taken more seriously than our small size alone indicated. This bear began making himself scarce. Another I used the same technique on seemed to stop coming around altogether. Others appear to have taken their place.

One night a pair of bears was fishing off the weir. They crouch on its upstream side and grab fish that stray too close. One must have felt like his turf was being invaded, for at intervals throughout the night we heard roars and deep growls that simply pierced us with terror: an instinctive, primitive gut reaction no doubt inherited from our distant, cave-dwelling, forebears. I was glad it was not directed at me!!

I went down to investigate at one point and stood on the weir gazing across. The two beasts were at the other end, forty yards away. Their eyes glowed bright orange. Just as I turned to go, one apparently rushed the other, letting fly one of those lionlike roars, deep and penetrating, that nearly froze me on the spot. What lungs! It was an effort to turn around and face them and make sure it wasn't me that was being charged.

We were exploring a stream for spawning salmon one day and I had just emerged from a tangle of fallen trees. Suddenly I saw four bears, a mom and three large cubs—just the instant they saw me. My first reaction was that it was a regular crowd of furry creatures. I felt like I was in a minority! Fortunately, they roared away in the other direction.

I really wish I hadn't scared them so that I could have observed them awhile. Do they share food? Fight? Play? How closely does Mama supervise or protect them at that age? She'll be kicking them out on their own next spring or summer anyway.

And so, like countless wilderness enthusiasts before me, I dwell at length on grizzly bears. There is no doubt they make more of an impression on you than just about any other creature in North America. Wolves do much the same thing to a person's heart, but there are no wolves around here that I've heard or heard of. (For some reason, neither wolves nor black bears are found on the so-called ABC islands of southeast Alaska—Admiralty, Baranof, and Chichagof. It also happens that these three are inhabited by brown bears. It's tempting to think that this is not just a coincidence, but on the mainland anyway, they are not all mutually exclusive. That is, brown bears, black bears, and wolves can all occur in the same area.)

Without the bears, this country would not be genuine wilderness; the cast in God's great play would be deprived of one of its leading characters. There would be something essential lacking, just as a death in a family leaves it fragmented forever, incomplete, wanting.

If the bear were to disappear like the Indian before it, these forests would lose much of their spirit, at least to the sensitive human soul. I doubt if the ducks on our lake would care very much. Fortunately, since these parts are set aside as a National Wilderness Area, it's not likely the bears will lose their habitat. Hunting is also regulated, so they won't be shot into oblivion like they have been elsewhere, barring some unforeseeable collapse of authority. I've heard that the number of grizzlies left in the world may number only twenty to thirty thousand, or less than the population of many small towns. So we've proved just who rules; now it's time to be benevolent in victory. I feel privileged to have seen so many grizzlies wild and free, and I hope that humankind will have the wisdom and generosity to allow them to endure into the next millennium and beyond.

Love,
Leon

*

November 12   *noon water level 72.5 centimeters*
                                 noon water temp. 39 degrees F

Weather: cool and overcast; no rain

The day began with a bang as we learned that Phil will be out tomorrow and as we realized the project is rapidly coming to an end.

We walked downstream all the way to saltwater today, to make as careful an estimate as we could of the number of cohos in the river below the weir. Between the weir and the main waiting pool there were 171 cohos, perhaps a dozen or two of which appeared to be spawning. In the pool itself I counted 136. Below the pool we counted 53 cohos, presumably all spawners. Undoubtedly there were others hidden that we did not see, so this should be considered a conservative estimate.

November 13   *3 P.M. water level 74 centimeters*
                        11:45 P.M. water level about 90 centimeters
                                 noon temp. 38.5 degrees F

Weather: misting rain & gusts much of day; poor visibility; evening—harder rain. Must be snowing above, because water level seems unresponsive.

Phil had planned to come in today, but the weather showed again it has no regard for mere mortal plans: It dumped on us in true southeast Alaska spirit.

We confined ourselves to camp all day, preparing cargo for a plane that never came. Word from Leon is that Monday the 15th is the earliest to expect Phil. At least we can bask beside the oven a couple of more nights.

No fish movement at the weir today.

Saw a bear on weir late at night. Zapped 'im with my flashlight beam and he hurried away like a wimpy mousie instead of the big bully he was.

November 14   *noon water level 103 centimeters*
                                       noon water temp. 39 degrees F

Weather: overcast with intermittent hail and rain; wind becalmed

Hit the creeks again today, hoping to see some spawners in higher water. Stream A did not have as many spawners as it has had on other occasions, but we still managed to net up 12. We walked only about 300 yards on Stream B and saw only 1 fish in that distance. The moderately high water made it difficult to see, so we cut out and headed over to Stream D. There we saw 3–4 cohos and nabbed one.

Still see gulls flying along spawning streams through the woods, looking out of place in such deep forest.

There are a number of small flocks of waterfowl on the lake these days. The Arctic must be turning even more inhospitable than this region.

November 15   *noon water level 90 centimeters*
                                       6 P.M. water temp. 39 degrees F

Weather: rained gently much of last night. When the clouds thinned this morning, the mountains appeared freshly arrayed in new snow—very magnificent. Turned into a cool, mostly clear day.

The mercury is probably already below 32 degrees F as I write this at 7 P.M., and for the first time in a while, we feel it, for our beloved stove is disconnected. Am writing this in gloves. I have cold feet and damp socks that I'm trying to dry over the lanterns—a slow, slow process. We droop them over the upright lantern handle and the lower parts get singed while above it hardly warms at all. The aroma of burning wool fills the cabin.

Squandered the day again preparing for a plane that never came. Phil did manage to reach us in early P.M. from Sitka to say that the pilot will try to land him here at 8:30 A.M. tomorrow. We have carried just about everything we intend to ship out on this flight to a gravel bar toward the middle of the lake and covered the pile with the tent fly. Hope there are no more aborted plans or bear "investigations."

I slept in my own tent last night and thought or imagined I heard bear growls. The tight nylon fly is like a drum when raindrops strike it, so with the steady drumroll I couldn't be sure, but when I poked my head out and scanned with the flashlight, sure enough, there flickered the telltale orange eyes 30 yards away. Scarcely a night passes that we don't see or hear bears, and even on those we don't, I'm sure they're nosing around somewhere nearby.

November 16   *no temp./water level recorded*

Weather: clear, cold, & blustery

Phil arrived today and with him the clear, sunny weather, in keeping with his past visits. His last name ought to be Blue, not Gray!

We checked all 4 streams today and managed to shag 7 spawning cohos. Saw between 5–10 fish on Stream A; 10–15 on Stream B; and none on the other two. I returned separately along Stream A to retrieve the boat at one point and saw 4 otters in the lake from A's mouth, their heads resembling miniature seals', and their bodies undulating like sea serpents.

Meanwhile, Phil and Detlef surprised a sow and 2 cubs along Stream B. They managed to escape being chewed on, although for a moment it looked like Big Mama was moving in for the kill. Phil and Detlef chose flight over fight, which was wise, since they didn't have the gun. In his frantic dash to get away, Phil dropped his cap in the stream, although Detlef was able to fish it out for him after the danger had passed. Later, Detlef expressed amazement at how fast Phil could run with a bear on his heels! Afterward, it all seemed more like a cartoon than a life-threatening ordeal. Our ability to pass so quickly from fright to laughter is remarkable.

November 18

Weather: continuing clear, cold, windy. The winds have scarcely paused in 3–4 days now. We were startled to see ice forming in the bay in front of camp this morning. Later we observed that most of the southern, shallow end of the lake (toward camp) was in fact frozen over with a layer of thin ice.

Yesterday, Phil walked to saltwater and made a final count of the cohos remaining below the weir. He counted 54 from the weir to the pool, 275 in the pool, and 5 below the pool, for a total of 334. This compares with our estimate of 361 on November 12. (Since then, 10 fish have come through the weir.) The estimates are within 10% of each other, and it makes sense that there are fewer fish now anyway. We're satisfied.

We started dismantling the weir at about noon. By darkfall (about 5 P.M.) we had removed all the pickets (over 900 including trap), the chicken wire, catwalk, and most of the channel. Today we carried up and stacked the 18 tripods, trap components, and miscellany. The entire job took about 10 hours. We left the sandbags in place. Those tripods above water were stuck in frozen ground and had to be sledgehammered and pried free. Looks as though the weir wasn't jerked a moment too soon!

The freezing lake has necessitated a change in plans. We were intending on leaving early tomorrow morning, but the floatplane can't land on the lake anymore (safely). It has floats, not skis. So we will try to float our load in the raft down to saltwater tomorrow for a pickup the following morning. We have a lot to get out, not the least 3 shivering bodies!

*

November 18, 1982
Thursday

Dear Folks,

I'm discovering why Alaska has a reputation as "the howling north." A savage north wind has hardly paused in four days. Coupled with it is a clear sky with stars that crinkle in the frigid nights.

We are now dismantling the weir. This morning we were startled to see the lake freezing. We were supposed to be picked up tomorrow morning, but the floatplane can no longer land on the lake in its present state. So, we will have to load up the raft and float it the mile down to the ocean. The only problem is that a number of logs block the way so we'll have to load and unload the raft an equal number of times. Tomorrow night we'll camp on the beach. Then with good luck the plane will retrieve us at Ford Arm itself the next morning.

The weather can be so heartless . . . I've found myself thinking of Jack London stories all day during our cold toil.

Tonight on the lakeshore I played my last rendition of taps. The notes had a more melancholy ring to them than ever. . . .

November 20, 1982
Saturday

Our last full day at Ford Arm, Friday the 19th, became more of a pain in the buttocks than we could have ever imagined. It dawned with the disturbing discovery that not only the lake, but the stream itself was freezing up on us. This could have prevented our rafting our supplies down, which would have necessitated our portaging the entire load the entire distance to tidewater. This was about one mile of bushwhacking through thick brush, over logjams, and along slippery rocks.

Since we had a plane pickup arranged for early Saturday morning, it began to look like we would each have to make about ten carries (twenty miles altogether) in a single short day if we were to make it out in time. If it had been a simple matter of just carrying ten fifty-pound backpacks along a cleared trail I would've tackled it with gusto. These, however, were very awkward loads—the chain saw, generator, duffel bags, the raft itself, etc.—the sort that exhaust your arms every hundred yards, especially when dragging them through thick brush and over logs.

I felt demoralized at the thought of all the mind-numbing hours of cheerless, brute work in front of us. Knowing that if my boss Phil were willing to spend a few more bucks (well, actually quite a few more bucks!) for a helicopter that could land right at camp and eliminate all carrying didn't help my outlook. Nor did the eager, let's-go-get-em attitudes of both Detlef and Phil toward carrying everything out in our arms; their naiveté or their strength, whichever it was, annoyed me.

We hastily finished up the remaining steps in closing down the camp for the season—stripping the tent roof and fly off its frame, bringing down the SSB radio antennae, and caching supplies and tools that we would leave behind under the wooden platform. This took longer than we anticipated of course, so by the time we were "saddled up" it was late afternoon. Only two hours, or less, of daylight remained. I grimly loaded up for what looked like the first of many carries. Detlef and I trudged down the faint bear path along the stream, cursing the hordes of alder branches that slapped our faces and threatened to poke our eyes. The only way to avoid them was by crawling, not very practical with our arms loaded up.

Well, we hadn't gone a hundred yards when Phil suddenly realized just how much work this was going to be. Hallelujah! So we piled everything into the raft and decided to try floating it downstream, despite the one to two inches of ice buildup on the surface. Wearing our chest waders, Detlef and I walked ahead of the raft in the hip-deep water breaking the ice sheet into cakes by stomping it with our heavy rubber boots. Phil walked the raft behind us and in this way we advanced a foot at a time. If the ice had been a centimeter thicker, I doubt if we could have broken it and we would have been forced ashore. Now our chief worry was puncturing the rubber raft or our waders on some sharp edge of ice.

We were able to proceed about a hundred yards before encountering the first of many fallen logs barring our passage. To get the raft over, we first had to unload it; then we could lift it up and over and load it again and float another twenty yards before repeating the procedure at the next log. Fortunately, the logjams weren't spaced this way the whole distance! To cover a log-free fifty yards might take ten minutes; to cover the same distance with two logs to cross at least half an hour.

But this wasn't the worst of it. We then began running into stretches too shallow to raft, which forced us to do long portages. This was the slowest going of all, for instead of being able to float the whole load down in one trip (and not carry anything in our arms), we would each have to make about ten strenuous trips. So on these stretches we were literally ten times as slow.

Daylight faded to twilight, and the twilight to night, but we couldn't afford to stop if we were to meet our plane. If we missed it there was no telling when we'd get out. When our sight failed in the darkness, we lit a lantern, which one person carried while the other two lugged gear. About 8:00 P.M. we flopped onto a gravel bar and indulged in a cracker, cheese, and cookie snack.

Rejuvenated, we hit it again and continued on until 11:30 P.M., before stopping for the night on another gravel bar. We thought we were within easy range of meeting our plane in the morning; the tidal meadow was only a quarter-mile away. With the stream tumbling past several yards away, and the stars peeping down on us from the far reaches of the galaxy, I settled into my sleeping bag for what was to be my final night in the bush, too weary to worry about bears stumbling over us, or to feel the hard, lumpy stones underneath.

We hopped into action again an hour before sunrise, when the first silhouettes of trees loomed visible against the dim gray sky. There was no time to dally over breakfast.

The last quarter-mile was a real grunt, the worst stretch of all. It was too shallow and rocky to raft and the banks were too steep for any trail, so we were forced to carry the whole shebang over slippery rocks and through the water. Again and again I trudged the same route, burning out steadily, but happy to see the pile of things to be carried shrink with each return.

Twice I slipped and nearly fell into the frigid water, but I caught myself in time and soaked only my wrists. I had finally succeeded in puncturing a tiny hole in the chest waders and felt cold water oozing onto my ankle and down into my foot. It squished with each step. Detlef had long since punctured both of his boots, and he covered each leg with a plastic garbage bag before putting his boots on.

I marveled at Phil's and Detlef's stamina and relatively chipper spirits; I felt spent and grumpy, like a beaten dog. I was actually a bit irritated at Detlef's good mood, because I knew that in good part it was due to the fact that within a few hours he would be reunited with his wife after three months away. No one awaited me with open arms and leaping heart. All I felt at the thought of returning, now that it was upon me, was uneasiness and a vague sense of estrangement.

After twelve hours of slave labor, at long last the final leg was behind us. I was absolutely trashed. Just as we began deflating the raft, we heard the telltale drone of an approaching plane. This time the engine's noisy greeting carried more than a hint of just food and mail—now it signified the end of our exile in the wilds of southeast Alaska.

The pilot landed and taxied over to us. I was afraid his four-seater Beaver wouldn't accommodate our mountainous load, but we managed to squeeze it all in and still find barely enough space to fit in ourselves. The pilot told us that he saw the lake as he flew over and that he could have landed and taken off on the half that was still open, so that our backpacking trek was probably unnecessary after all. I should have been upset, but I was too exhausted and too anxious about returning to civilization to care.

Love,
Leon

Farewell to Ford Arm

Juneau, Alaska
November 23, 1982
Tuesday

Dear Folks,

I'm back in town after fifteen weeks away. Alaska has a new governor, a new legislature, but the same capital. The voters elected to leave it in Juneau after all. My friends the Dunkers have moved. The mountains haven't moved, but are dressed in their white winter garb. The world keeps turning, and I have to catch up on much. I must have thirty unopened business and job-related letters to attend to. It's almost as overwhelming as my first week at Ford Arm.

Last Saturday was tumultuous. Before dawn I lay congealed in my sleeping bag beside a half-frozen wilderness stream. A vault of brittle, sparkling stars light years away was the only roof over my head. Before the day ended, two plane flights had carried me away to two towns and a frenzy of human activity. On the second plane, a commercial Alaska Airlines flight, a stranger who was assigned the seat beside mine soon got up and moved away. He didn't say anything, but I suspect my more than three months without a bath had something to do with it. And I had even put on my least smelly wool sweater as a concession to civilization!

My first face-to-face encounter with those I now call "other" people (i.e., anyone other than Detlef and me) was on the main street of Sitka, the old capital of Russian America, where three born-again Christians waylaid me and preached the message of their lord and savior. I nodded dutifully but was capable of only monosyllabic responses and a dazed expression. Eventually they seemed to conclude that I was brain damaged, because they found an excuse to move away.

That same night, back in Juneau, after surprising John Dunker and Amy Paige for dinner, I ran into a friend who dragged me around town, introducing me to at least a dozen strangers and explaining to them just why I seemed shy or incommunicative. The provocatively dancing women, the flowing booze, and the hazy air in the disco he hauled me to were practically nauseating. One woman was wearing face paint (I think it's called makeup) that she must've thought enhanced her looks, but I thought all the red on her cheeks made her look like a clown instead. Anyway, she seemed curious about my recent experience, but I was too timid to look her in the eye more than a split second, and my halting words were drowned in the blaring music. How plaintive, yet how choice, Detlef's harmonica sounded by comparison to these screaming and squealing electric guitars!

I have since found out something about my first partner, Dan Hutchins. After he left me, Dan volunteered at another weir on Klakas Lake down on Prince of Wales Island for another couple of months. At one point, Fish and Game had to fly an unscheduled plane into Klakas to remove Dan's partner. That's the verifiable fact of the situation. The rumor, that could be so easily perpetuated behind the back of someone like Dan, was that he had threatened to kill his partner. He was said to have stalked around the outside of their cabin firing his .44 Magnum into the air to let his partner know he was displeased. When I ran into Dan and asked him about this, he claimed they mutually agreed that it would be a good idea if his partner left.

It's the rumor people will remember, though, because it's more sensational and because Dan is not the sort to stick up for himself. Another incident occurred when Dan tried to board an Alaska Airlines flight with his holstered .44 Magnum strapped to his waist. Of course the X-ray caught it and a state trooper stepped over, whereupon Dan flashed a badge, said he worked for Fish and Game, and that the gun was for bear protection. He also gave our boss Phil Gray's name.

Well, he had no authority to be carrying a badge and the one he had probably came from a Cracker Jacks box or some other less-than-official source. The state trooper said he could have arrested him right there for impersonating an officer, but instead he contacted Phil Gray, who was less than pleased. Dan later claimed he'd been led to believe that carrying the gun on board was okayed by some Alaska Airlines person, but obviously, that person must not have understood him, or vice versa. You simply *don't do that!*

This incident is a telling example of Dan's poor judgment and grasp of social conventions. The tragedy is that it had to be noted on his work record and that it alone is probably sufficient to ruin his dream, that of becoming a candidate for the Fish and Game warden training school. I've heard since that Dan is slinging soup to the down-and-out at a Christian-run diner called the Glory Hole.

My other partner, Detlef Büttner, was met at the airport in Juneau by his pretty wife with a bottle of wine in her hand and a twinkle in her eye. Detlef too hadn't bathed in months, but that didn't deter her. As they walked off arm in arm, I felt envy's green lick. No lover awaited me with open arms, sparkling eyes, and mischief up her sleeve.

Unfortunately, the story doesn't end happily ever after, as I discovered when I bumped into Detlef on the street a couple of days later. The three months apart, which he had hoped would make the heart grow fonder, had not benefited his marriage. He looked very troubled. I didn't envy him any longer. Love stinks.

Detlef gave me a gift, a photo of me that I never even realized he took, because my back was to the camera. We were standing in an open meadow at the edge of Ford Arm. I was dressed in dark green rain gear, gun in one hand and walking stick in the other. I was watching a bald eagle take off from the ground. It was misty, and that imparted such a softness to the photo that at first I thought it might be one of Detlef's own watercolor renderings.

It has such a mystical quality; better than any of my own photos, it captures the wonder of this wilderness and our own intimate relationship with it. On the back Detlef wrote:

Hey Mister Muir!
Resting on your cane again?
Where are crackers and wool blanket? Yes, Sir
The season is right
When the snow comes . . .

I cherish both the photo and Detlef's evocative words.

My readjustment to the jarring sights, sounds, faces, and changes of civilization has been more painful than I envisioned. In a sense, I feel more isolated than I was at Ford Arm. *Already I miss it.*

Again and again I recall one particular night when I walked anxiously down to the weir to investigate yet again a bloodcurdling medley of roars, grunts, and growls. Two sets of orange eyes glared back into my flashlight beam until one set blinked out as one bruin turned to face its adversary. Satisfied that we humans weren't the target of these menacing bellows, I turned to go. Just then, my eyes caught sight of the northern lights above the black mountain at the far end of the lake. Curtains and ribbons of eerie green light swayed and twisted silently as charged particles riding the solar wind performed their cosmic waltz in the Earth's upper atmosphere. I stood for awhile, spellbound, watching the mysterious aurora borealis and listening to the two brown bears rumble across the stream. And I thought to myself, *this* is quintessential Alaska.

Earlier I wrote that I thought I'd be babbly and expansive when I made my return debut. I was wrong. It's just the opposite. I feel withdrawn and socially inept. I can't hold another person's eyes easily, especially those of the opposite gender. I feel out of place in small gatherings (to say nothing of smoky discotheques).

The paths around Ford Arm Lake, the muddy trail to the outhouse, the steps of our cabin, the weir, the dying cohos, the bears, the ravens, the fearless deer, the starry nights, the sounds of the night—all reappear if I shut my eyes—so real. But only a short time ago I was there. Soon these vivid visions will fade to memories—precious, precious memories.

I would have said, "Farewell Ford Arm Lake!" but I don't want the working name we stuck you with to become permanent. Naming is the start of taming. I want you to stay wild and obscure as you have for aeons, across ice ages and interglacials. At the end of my life, I want to be able to scan the latest USGS quadrangle of western Chichagof Island and see that the lake feeding the principal stream flowing into Ford Arm still has no name. Farewell wild lake!

Epilogue

A decade has now slipped by and my path through life has led me far from the bear trails I once trod through thickets of devil's club on Chichagof Island. I haven't seen my old companions Dan and Detlef in many a year now.

Dan left Alaska in the early eighties for more southerly realms of the Pacific Northwest. The last time I spoke with him was by telephone in Seattle. I am sorry to report that he never became an Alaska game warden. I wish him well in his present endeavors, whatever they are, and hope that at last he may have found a calling in life. I often wonder if his ex-wife ever allowed him to truly be a father to the daughter of whom he spoke tenderly to me. She would now be a young woman. It would be nice to know she got to see her dad every so often, but from what Dan used to say, I'm not hopeful.

Detlef remained in Alaska, graduating eventually with a fisheries management degree from the University of Alaska in Juneau. He works for the Alaska Department of Fish and Game at a lab in town, only now as a salaried employee instead of a volunteer. The year after he returned from Ford Arm, his wife gave birth to a baby boy. Unfortunately, however, their marriage didn't last. Detlef went on to develop his artistic talent for illustrating and painting Alaskan fish and has even attained a measure of recognition and commercial success. Leon Shaul tells me he has seen Detlef's framed paintings hanging on office walls in Juneau.

After my sojourn at Chichagof Island in 1982, I continued to work for the Coho Research Project of the Alaska Department of Fish and Game until 1985. In fact, I even returned to Ford Arm once more the following spawning season for three months, only this time with a female partner. We relived many of the adventures and misadventures from the previous autumn with salmon, bears, and floods. We also experienced one wholly new adventure—romance. But that's another story.

Overall, we at Coho Research tagged and studied wild stocks of both adult and juvenile coho salmon at a number of remote sites scattered across the Alaska panhandle. I roamed from rain-drenched Misty Fiords National Monument at the southern tip, to the very northern edge of the region at Yakutat, where immense glaciers and the eternal snows of majestic Mt. Saint Elias preside with grandeur and Pleistocene serenity.

In 1985 I made a fateful decision I still feel wistful about years later: to depart Alaska and join the Peace Corps. For years I had had a long-standing desire to live in another country and culture, learn a new language, and promote natural-resource conservation in a "developing" nation. This restless longing eventually eclipsed even my abiding fondness for living and working in the northern wilderness. So I abandoned Alaska and the shivering subarctic for Honduras and the sweating subtropics, but not without a good deal of regret and many backward glances, which continue to this day.

I remained in Honduras until 1988, and my experiences there were very rewarding, both professionally and personally. Professionally, I worked as a technical advisor to the Honduran Ecological Association, a nonprofit organization waging an uphill struggle for the protection of the country's dwindling natural flora and fauna. I helped lead research expeditions into the exuberant tropical rain forests and rugged mountains of the Cordillera Nombre de Dios. (There the chief fear was not grizzly bears but poisonous snakes.) These efforts and others assisted in the establishment of Pico Bonito National Park, near the town of La Ceiba on the Caribbean Coast of Honduras. I vacillate between guarded optimism and slumping pessimism over whether the Honduran government and people can withstand the human greed and need that increasingly besiege this and other vestiges of wild nature in the country.

Personally, I had the pleasure of residing in a lively Caribbean port for a couple of years—La Ceiba. Named for a towering tree, this town is often referred to as *Ceibita la bella* (beautiful little Ceiba). It was a place that I felt certain Hemingway would have liked, for the mountains and tropical flora, the sea, the nearby islands, the coral reefs and fishing, the bars, and of course the women. I learned *español* and made many friends.

It is not torturing the truth to say that Honduras, like Alaska, changed me forever. Though I left, I took a piece of it with me: I am now married to a Honduran, the former Ana Veronica Castillo Gutierrez. Her shining eyes cast a spell over me the moment we met at the 1987 La Ceiba Carnival. This annual celebration is one of those rousing street festivals the Caribbean is renowned for, with live music and dancing under the stars from dusk till dawn. As the day broke, Vero and I waded into the balmy sea and watched the sun rise on a new era in our lives. In 1989 we were married in Albuquerque, New Mexico. The vows were bilingual, so that my newly arrived Spanish-speaking bride could comprehend what she was getting into. Three years later, in 1992, we welcomed a baby boy into our family.

For two years after our return from Honduras we lived with a sister of mine in Albuquerque, in the high desert of northern New Mexico at the edge of the Rockies. While pursuing certification as a high school science teacher, I tutored at the University of New Mexico library and made a concerted effort to explore as much as possible of the state that bills itself as "The Land of Enchantment." Poor economically, New Mexico is indeed wealthy in natural and human heritage. Its sweeping landscape is timeless and full of secrets whispered in the wind; its rich tricultural past and present are every bit as colorful as the land.

In 1990 I was offered and took a position as an environmental planner for the County of Orange in Santa Ana, California, between Los Angeles and San Diego. Southern California is a region whose seaside environment and comfortable climate are both a blessing and a curse. Those qualities drew millions of Americans here. These immigrants in turn created a dynamic economy that continues to lure millions more from around the world. If lately there are signs of a faltering economy, there is no hint of a slowdown in California's mushrooming population growth. Yet the state is already staggering under the burden of too many people and too many cars. Overpopulation will crush this land of limousines and low-riders before earthquakes ever do.

Of course, one could adopt the perspective of my old boss in Alaska: The more people are packed into California, the longer wilderness holdouts like Alaska can remain thinly populated and wild. "Your sacred mission as a planner," he wrote, "is to keep California just livable enough that those 30 million people won't move north!" But it's already happening, as Oregon and Washington can attest.

When I am stuck sitting in a traffic jam on one of Southern California's infamous freeways, whether from nostalgia or too much tailpipe exhaust, my mind often wanders back to the Alaskan wilderness I once lived in. What has become of the lake at Ford Arm, the cohos, and the bears in the years since I last saw them? It reassures me to know that little has changed. Phil Gray has retired, but Leon Shaul, who now directs Coho Research, keeps me apprised of what goes on at my beloved lake.

Since we started it, the coho weir at Ford Arm has been up and running every fall but one. Several other teams have faithfully tended the operation since my own stints there. Shaul is accumulating a small library of the logs, journals, and accounts kept over the years by different weir-hands, from mundane lists to literary reflections.

Because of the constant danger posed by a massive limb hanging precariously above it, our original wall-tent frame was dismantled and rebuilt a short distance away several years back. This time it was constructed by someone with a genuine knowledge of carpentry, and it is said to be sturdier, cozier, more functional, and even prettier than when two know-nothings first whacked it together haphazardly in August of 1982.

Leon assures me that the lake and the area around it are unchanged, as isolated and wild as I remember them. The escapement of spawning adult coho salmon into "Ford Arm Lake" has stayed remarkably consistent over the past decade, roughly twenty-three hundred fish. That means over four million eggs are laid annually and that each spring about one million tiny new cohos wriggle into being. It's a regular fish factory, and because its National Wilderness Area status keeps it from ever being logged, there is every reason to hope that it will stay productive well into the future.

Beyond the boundaries of this one basin, however, the outlook for the coho and other Pacific salmon is not as bright. Logging within the Tongass National Forest that comprises most of southeast Alaska will continue to take its toll, although conservationists have been partially successful in containing the damage. A number of large mines recently opened or proposed throughout Southeast also pose some threat in certain areas. Still, Alaska as a whole continues to enjoy historically high salmon harvests, though a fraction of this can be attributed to artificial fish hatcheries instead of natural production.

Outside Alaska, neighboring British Columbia's salmon stocks have long suffered from a combination of overfishing and rapacious logging. In Washington, Oregon, and California, certain runs of chinook and sockeye salmon are so decimated from a combination of logging, dams, irrigation projects, land development, and pollution that they have been proposed for protection under the Endangered Species Act. Here, hatcheries have assumed a major role in perpetuating the species. The undisturbed productive wild habitat for spawning and rearing is just too shrunken and inaccessible. In 1992, in a desperate effort to save these salmon stocks, the Pacific Fisheries Management Council imposed unprecedented and painful restrictions on the commercial and recreational salmon harvest.

Out on the high Pacific, Asian boats have been accused of intercepting U.S.-
and Canadian-bred fish with their drift nets. By the late eighties, tens of
thousands of miles of gill nets were set drifting in the Pacific each night, slaugh-
tering far more than just salmon. Happily, international outrage at this senseless
massacre appears to be forcing these nations to back off, albeit reluctantly.

I am pleased to report the brown bears continue in force at Ford Arm.
My successors have each had their share (or fill!) of them. Each year, certain
bears become regular visitors to the weir. Other bears remain merely a shadowy
presence, seen rarely or encountered only through their footprints, clawmarks,
and scat. The grizzly population appears healthy, though characterized by the
fluctuations in size noted in most wild-animal populations. I often wonder if
some of the very same bears I saw are still plodding up and down Ford Arm's
shores and stream banks. Since brown bears have been known to survive twenty
years or more, it is quite possible.

Elsewhere, the news is generally good for Alaskan grizzlies. An estimated
thirty-five thousand roam the state's forests and tundra, a population that
biologists consider healthy and stable. The Canadian wilds also continue to
support fairly large numbers. In the lower 48, however, the situation for grizzlies
is grim. The species clings to existence only in Montana, Wyoming, and perhaps
Idaho, and its grip on survival is precarious. In California, where grizzlies once
lived, the only place they now survive is on the state flag.

Ten years ago at Ford Arm, I remember thinking it would be boring to
go hiking anywhere else without brown bears. The constant thrill and threat
of a potential grizzly encounter enlivened each hike there. I relished walking
close to the edge. Here in California, the forests devoid of grizzlies are safer
and more boring to stroll through now. Ironically, as the forests have become
tamer and safer, the streets have gotten wilder and more dangerous.

In my first year here in Southern California, I saw a man shot through
the back ten yards from me a mere block from my office, and, in a separate
incident, I was assaulted by an armed street gang. On the trails of virgin Alaska,
being ambushed by a grizzly was a possibility; on the streets of urban California,
being ambushed by some trigger-happy road warrior in a drive-by shooting
is also a possibility.

To be attacked by the largest species of the taxonomic order carnivora
is terrifying but somehow appropriate. To be attacked by the largest-brained
primate (and your own species at that!) is also terrifying, but pathetic, too.
Ironically, the urban wastelands left behind in the stampede of American

civilization toward some unattainable promised land of ever-increasing material plenty are more savage than the trampled wilderness they replace.

As a gauge of how deeply the hallowed grounds of Chichagof Island penetrated my soul and there left their mark, I still dream and daydream about Ford Arm a decade later. The daydreams are nostalgic reminiscences, but the dreams when I sleep at night are generally dark, filled with a sense of doom. In them I see this natural shrine despoiled or developed. And that fear is at least partly irrational, because Ford Arm does lie within a National Wilderness Area. It would take literally an Act of Congress to strip it of its protected status, although one can imagine readily the sorts of crises or national disintegration that might bring this about.

Alaska's governor is thought to be a one-man environmental crisis by many conservationists, and the state's congressional delegation hardly an improvement — prodevelopment boomers all. They accept no federally protected land as entirely off limits to so-called progress. Their ambition for the future of the "last frontier" is a nightmare for those of us who treasure Alaska's abundant natural resources and untamed wilds for their own sake rather than merely as means to economic empire. These politicians or their allies could potentially find a way to undermine the safeguards of wilderness areas like Ford Arm.

One of the more recent schemes hatched by the boomers is the construction of a $110 billion pipeline to carry water from Alaska to the thirsty multitudes in California. (While it's at it, maybe the pipeline could carry salmon to California too, since they've been all but wiped out here.) Only the outrageous price tag has kept this proposal from more serious consideration. Other troubling scenarios abound. The limit of the wilderness area extends only to the edge of the Ford Arm watershed, a scant two miles or less from the lake. Logging could conceivably occur up to the very border, although I am informed that present harvesting plans for the Tongass National Forest do not call for this. Still, I wish I could be absolutely certain that someday the distant rumble of logging trucks and the whine of chain saws won't be mixed in with the growls of feuding brown bears.

Then there are the possible long-term and apocalyptic menaces, some of them hypothetical perhaps, but to me no less ominous for that: accidents like the *Exxon Valdez* oil spill, nuclear war, ozone depletion, induced global warming, and population growth in Alaska. Maybe a few years from now, the towns and tourist trade of the last frontier will have grown to the point that some entrepreneur will find it profitable to set up daily fishing or sight-seeing flights into Ford Arm (Whisk into the wilderness and back in an hour!). The scenery would remain, the solitude would not.

The grizzlies whose eyes we took pains to spare even while peppering them with birdshot may yet go blind anyway. If man-made chemicals (chlorofluoro-carbons) devour a hole in the Arctic's stratospheric ozone shield, as they already have done over Antarctica, potent ultraviolet-B radiation will rain down on the bears. Unlike us, they can't wear sunglasses. But the more likely possibility is that some of Ford Arm's brown bears will starve if the intensified UVB damages phytoplankton, photosynthesis, and the marine food chain. A smaller crop of phytoplankton ultimately means fewer salmon for bears to fatten on in order to survive the lean winters.

A promising future in perpetuity for the salmon, the bears, the ancient forest, and the solitude I came to cherish is by no means guaranteed. It is provisional. My harried spirit can still find sanctuary at Ford Arm . . . for the time being. In this rapidly changing, uncertain world, I'm afraid that's the most I can count on.